Everyman's Poetry

*Everyman, I will go with thee,
and be thy guide*

Lord Rochester

Edited with an introduction by PADDY LYONS

Professor of English, University of Warsaw

EVERYMAN

J. M Dent · London

Introduction and other critical apparatus
© J. M. Dent 1996

The moral right of Paddy Lyons
has been asserted.

All rights reserved

J. M. Dent
Orion Publishing Group
Orion House
5 Upper St Martin's Lane
London WC2H 9EA

Typeset by Deltatype Ltd, Ellesmere Port, Cheshire
Printed in Great Britain by
The Guernsey Press Co. Ltd, Guernsey, C.I.

This book if bound as a paperback is subject to the condition
that it may not be issued on loan or otherwise except
in its original binding

British Library Cataloguing-in-Publication
Data is available upon request.

ISBN 0 460 87819 0

Introduction

John Wilmot – second Earl of Rochester and third Viscount of Athlone – was born in Oxfordshire on 1 April 1647, and died there on 26 July 1680, notorious because – as Samuel Johnson put it – 'he blazed out his youth and health in lavish voluptuousness'. Rochester's mother was Parliamentarian by descent, and inclined to Puritanism. His father, a hard-drinking Royalist from Anglo-Irish stock, had been created Earl of Rochester in 1652 for military services to Charles II during his exile under the Commonwealth; he died abroad in 1658, two years before the restoration of monarchy in England.

At twelve Rochester matriculated at Wadham College, Oxford, and there, it is said, 'grew debauched'. At fourteen he was conferred with the degree of M.A. by the Earl of Clarendon, who was Chancellor to the University and Rochester's uncle. After a tour of France and Italy, Rochester returned to London, where he was to grace the Restoration Court. Courage in sea-battle against the Dutch made him a hero. In 1667 he married Elizabeth Malet, a witty heiress whom he had attempted to abduct two years earlier.

Rochester's life is divided between domesticity in the country and a riotous existence at Court, where he was renowned for drunkenness, vivacious conversation, and extravagant 'frolics'. In banishment from Court for a scurrilous lampoon on Charles II, Rochester set up as 'Doctor Bendo', a physician skilled in treating barrenness; his practice was, it is said, 'not without success'. Deeply involved with theatre, his coaching of his mistress Elizabeth Barry began her career as the greatest actress of the Restoration stage. At the age of thirty-three, as Rochester lay dying – from syphilis, it is assumed – his mother had him attended by her religious associates; a death-bed renunciation of atheism was published and promulgated as the conversion of a prodigal. This became legendary, reappearing in numerous pious tracts over the next two centuries. Rochester's own writings were at once admired and infamous. Posthumous printings of his play *Sodom, or the Quintessence of Debauchery* gave rise to prosecutions for obscenity, and were destroyed. During his lifetime, his songs and satires were known mainly from anonymous broadsheets and manuscript circulation; most of Rochester's poetry was not published under his name until after his death.

One of the most accessible and attractive of the major English poets, Rochester has long been the least available. Though his poetry is as persistently literary as it is lively, it has been marginalised by the very forces which gathered and gave profile to the writings that compose English Literature. Rochester has not lacked distinguished admirers. Defoe quoted him widely and often. Tennyson would recite from him with fervour. Voltaire admired Rochester's satire for 'energy and fire' and translated some lines into French to 'display the shining imagination his lordship only could boast'. Goethe could quote Rochester in English, and cited his lines to epitomise the intensely 'mournful region' he encountered in English poetry. Hazlitt judged that 'his verses cut and sparkle like diamonds', while 'his contempt for everything that others respect almost amounts to sublimity'.[1] Pope studied with care Rochester's adaptations of Latin poetry, but himself wrote a stiff and dismissive poem 'On lying in the Earl of Rochester's bed at Atterbury'. But from roughly the mid-eighteenth century until roughly the second quarter of this century, the small poetic output of Rochester's brief life was, at best, available in carefully pruned-down selections, and more often represented by a handful of anthologised pieces. Until relatively recently the full range of his poetry remained uncollected, and his notorious play, *Sodom* – once burned by the public hangman – was unavailable to readers.[2] But while it is often obvious who the text-police might have been working for, the actual standards whereby Rochester has been outlawed are not quite always those which are professed.

The philosopher Spinoza – a contemporary of Rochester – took it as axiomatic that the word 'dog' cannot bark: 'A true idea (for we possess a true idea) is something different from its correlate (ideatum); thus a circle is different from the idea of a circle . . . nor is the idea of a body that body itself.'[3] But in England, Spinoza's gentle equanimity did not prevail and, within a decade or so of Rochester's death, words pertaining to the body became a focus for excited outrage among custodians of culture. In 1691 a collection of Rochester's poems was published by the bookseller Jacob Tonson, also the publisher of Dryden and Milton and, arguably, 'the arranger, possibly the inventor, of the accepted canon of English literature until very recently'.[4] Tonson's edition was prefaced with a reassurance that the publisher had 'been diligent out of measure ... that every Block of Offence shou'd be removed'. Thus, for example, the final line of Rochester's Anacreontic, following Ronsard' (p. 66 below) was altered to read 'And thence to Love again', Tonson's four letter word 'Love' replacing Rochester's word 'cunt'. In the drive for decency, willingness to expunge counted for more than any awareness of how expurgation can itself create improprieties. In Tonson's version, 'Fair Cloris in a pigsty lay' (p. 41 below) appeared minus its last stanza, and 'the excision of the final stanza in order to remove a reference to female masturbation converts a dream of rape, which is offensive enough in all consequence, into an actual rape'.[5] Taking the word for the thing – hearing 'dog' bark – and then manifesting decency through deletion, has continued to mangle editions of Rochester.[6] According to the preface to Vivian de Sola Pinto's 1953 edition of Rochester, two poems – 'A Ramble in St James's Park' and 'The Imperfect Enjoyment' (p. 51 and p. 55 below) – 'had to be omitted at the request of the publishers owing to the risk of prosecution in this country under the existing law'.[7]

Self-congratulation rather than self-enquiry is most commonly the stance that censors take. 'Two little books,' wrote Virginia Woolf of D. H. Lawrence's poetry 'which read like the sayings that small boys scribble upon stiles to make housemaids jump and titter'[8] – and by letting it be seen how the policing of words is visibly entwined with class bias, respectability here lays bare its involvement with snobbishness. As William Empson noted, his more assured class position enabled Rochester to discourse in broader registers:

> The reason why he could talk in this absolutely plain-man way was that he was a great lord and a favourite of the king: a person of lower class, such as a university professor or a Puritan preacher, would obviously have to talk in a more affected manner.[9]

Democratic plainness of language was, to Rochester's scientific contemporaries, a crucial prerequisite to serious thinking. In his *History of the Royal Society* (1667), Thomas Sprat observed in the scientists of the seventeenth-century a solicitousness 'about the manner of their discourse', a scrupulous sense that means shape ends, that exploratory argument is forwarded or disabled according to the kind of language in which it is conducted:

> They have exacted from all their members a close, naked, natural way of speaking; positive expressions, clear senses; a native easiness; bringing all things as near the Mathematical plainness, as they can: and preferring the language of Artizans, Countrymen, and Merchants, before that of Wits, or Scholars.[10]

By drawing into poetry plain terms to describe bodily parts and genital functions, Rochester's writing aligns itself with the egalitarian linguistic practices upheld in the name of clarity by the science of his era. He accords equal liberty of language to a duchess planning a night out on the town and a street-wise actress whom she consults:

> To some cellar in Sodom your Grace must retire,
> There porters with black pots sit round a coal fire.
> There open your case, and your Grace cannot fail
> Of a dozen of pricks, for a dozen of ale.
>
> Is't so? quoth the Duchess.
>
> > Aye by God, quoth the whore.
> Then give me the key that unlocks the back door –
> For I'd rather be fucked with porters and car-men
> Than thus be abused by Churchill and Jermyn.
>
> > ('Mistress Knight's Advice', p. 59 below)

This dialogue proposes a democracy of desire. If it is talk too uncouth to be entertained by 'such as a university professor or a Puritan preacher', and thus cannot be accommodated within English Literature, a question arises: how far are the boundaries of what is or is not 'literature' instituted on a class bias that disallows levelling?

Rochester is a poet of clear unbelief, of intelligent and vigorous doubt, of tensions that resist easy resolutions, and his poems have a tendency to put their own apparent assumptions into question. For example, 'Upon Nothing' (p. 25 below) starts out in a lofty championing of nihilism and uncreation, which has the bedrock assurance 'alone of ending unafraid'. Through a sequence of paradoxes, anti-matter serves as a touchstone against which the insecurities of temporality and materialism are found undesirable and are mocked. The satire extends into a consideration of linguistics, and the production of meaning through negative differentiation:

> Is or Is Not, the two great ends of Fate,
> And True or False, the subject of debate
> That perfect or destroy the vast designs of State –

> When they have racked the politician's breast,
> Within thy bosom most securely rest,
> And when reduced to thee are least unsafe and blessed.

Non-being is celebrated for the minimalist comfort it offers – 'least unsafe'. But then there is no pause, and instead of resting in the secure bosom of nihilism, the poem goes on to give linguistic manifestations of nothingness, to display nothingness in the meaninglessness of commonplaces and empty phrases:

> The great man's gratitude to his best friend,
> Kings' promises, whores' vows, towards thee they bend,
> Flow swiftly into thee, and in thee ever end.

Loftiness has given way to hollowness, and triteness is all. No more than in Rochester's extraordinary poems about impotence – tirades that veer unsettled between boastfulness and bathos – is there any of the sustained narcissistic poise of, for instance, Oscar Wilde's paradoxes. Instead, the poem has come full circle, disbelieving even disbelief, mobilising doubt until it counters itself. Nothing has been stated and, linguistically, actual nothingness has been demonstrated in all its unglory.

This is a poetry of restlessness, where any assertion is likely to be dismantled. Because it starts out from doubt, it assumes only what it can incorporate. Thus, with 'A Very Heroic Epistle in answer to Ephelia' (p. 24 below), there is no need for outside reading: what may have been put forward in the rejected woman's supposed complaint soon becomes evident in the course of this epistle's destructive progress. A discourse is at once evoked and opposed. Ephelia's excessive and heroic demands – which will get nowhere with someone whose stance is unabashedly self-centred – are speedily summarised, analysed, and disposed of:

> Well-mannered, honest, generous and stout –
> Names, by dull fools, to plague mankind found out.

The echo of her words evokes her sufficiently, and she can be dismissed as a nuisance, a discomfort, an annoying voice: 'For 'tis my maxim to avoid all pain'. Thus far, the mockery has been vicious but intelligent; next it goes on to fantasising, projecting into a state of absolute content where sexual gratification is luxuriantly free from any tedious requirement to answer back. The fantasy is at once vivid and quite tacky.

> Methinks I see thee underneath the shade
> Of golden canopies, supinely laid;
> Thy crouching slaves, all silent as the night,
> But at thy nod, all active as the light!
> Secure in solid sloth, thou there dost reign,
> And feel'st the joys of love, without the pain.

It is also cruelly vindictive, and the violence which went into humiliating Ephelia at a distance becomes, in imagination, brutally ruthless. Misogyny is out in the open:

> No loud reproach, nor fond unwelcome sound
> Of women's tongues, thy sacred ear dares wound.
> If any do, a nimble mute straight ties
> The true-love-knot, and stops her foolish cries.

But why, the poem continues, dream longingly of a state where love is secure from pain? – and then it arrives at an answer: the desire for security is propelled by its lack:

> Thou fear'st no injured kinsman's threatening blade,
> Nor midnight ambushes, by rivals laid.
> While here with aching heart, our joys we taste,
> Disturbed by swords, like Damocles his feast.

Again the ending turns back against the opening. Ephelia's unrealistic demands had been rebuked in the lucid idiom of everyday realism:

> . . . 'tis as natural to change, as love.
> You may as justly at the sun repine
> Because alike it does not always shine . . .

But it is only in fantasy that such realism can be put into action; in the here-and-now, the actual practice of such realism proves dangerous, impossible, boding only disaster and pain. There is a

boomerang effect as satire swings back against the hedonistic
ambition of the satirist ('to avoid all pain') again a circular
movement whereby all assertions are demolished, here leaving
only raw fear.

Much of the vitality of Rochester's poetry is in this constant
movement of inquiry into and past its own limits and boundaries.
'A Very Heroic Epistle' illustrates the troubles his critics have had in
attempting to establish Rochester's satiric stance. Biographical
criticism, assuming the first-person stance to correspond to that
held by the poet, accorded this poem 'the value of a self
confession'.[11] More ingeniously – perhaps even anticipating new
historicism – David Vieth argued that the poem's speaker is 'a
persona (that is, a dramatic speaker who is not strictly the same
person as the author) representing John Sheffield, Earl of Mulgrave,
whose conceit and self-sufficiency are satirised.'[12] But both of these
views presume a fixed stance, a stable distance between mockery
and its target – whether the distance is nil (as in 'self confession') or
involves a detachment (John Sheffield as an object of ridicule).
Neither view allows for the procedures of radical doubt which
destabilise distance, leaving the speaker's stance unfixed. However
Rochester is uniquely a non-didactic satirist, and it is these very
shifts of stance that make him at once such an energetic and very
hilarious poet, a writer who instead of settling for comfort preferred
the bleakness of ongoing honesty.

                                                    PADDY LYONS

Notes

1 *Rochester: The Critical Heritage*, ed. Farley-Hills (London: Routledge,
  1972) usefully anthologises critical comments before 1900.
2 A full text of *Sodom*, based on a new survey of early manuscripts, is
  included in *Rochester: Complete Poems and Plays*, edited by Paddy Lyons
  (Everyman, 1993). The difficult issues of authorship and attribution are
  discussed and re-examined in this edition, upon which the present text is
  based.
3 Baruch Spinoza, 'Treatise on the Improvement of the Understanding',
  transl. R. H. M. Elwes, *Works of Spinoza*, vol. 2 (London: Dover, 1955), p.
  12.
4 Keith Walker, 'Jacob Tonson, Bookseller,' in *The American Scholar*, vol.
  61 (3), 1992, p. 424.
5 Walker, ibid., p. 429.

6 A phenomenon examined and discussed thoroughly by James McGhee, 'Obscene Libel and the Language of "The Imperfect Enjoyment"', in *Reading Rochester*, ed. Edward Burns (Liverpool UP, 1995), pp. 42–65.

7 *Poems by John Wilmot, Earl of Rochester*, ed. Vivian de Sola Pinto (London: Routledge & Kegan Paul, 1953), p. xlix.

8 'Notes on D. H. Lawrence', in Virginia Woolf, *Collected Essays*, vol. 1, (London: Chatto & Windus, 1966), p. 352.

9 William Empson, 'Rochester', in *Argufying: Essays on Literature and Culture* ed. Haffenden (London: Hogart Press, 1988), p. 275.

10 Bishop Sprat's manifesto is quoted and discussed more fully by Basil Willey, *The Seventeenth Century Background* (London: Chatto & Windus, 1934), pp. 186–92.

11 Johannes Prinz, *John Wilmot, Earl of Rochester. His Life and Writings* (Leipzig: Palaestra, 1927), p. 212.

12 David M Vieth, *Attribution in Restoration Poetry: A Study of Rochester's 'Poems' of 1680* (New Haven & London: Yale University Press, 1963), p. 107.

Note on the Text

The aim of this volume is to make Rochester's poems available to contemporary readers, and the text here follows my Everyman edition of his *Complete Poems and Plays*. The order in which the poems appear is – by and large – that of their first known appearance in print. Thus, the first three poems here are juvenilia which were published under Rochester's name in 1660/1, when he was aged 13. The next thirteen pieces were published anonymously during Rochester's lifetime, and the remainder came into print variously and posthumously. Few of Rochester's poems can be dated with any exactitude, and attempts to construct even an approximate order of composition seem to me hopelessly speculative. Nor am I convinced by groupings of the poems according to theme or topic: Rochester's scepticism all too often turns the boundaries of genre inside out, so that satire can read like a backhanded tribute, while a declaration of feeling may become abstract investigation of a philosophical discourse.

Rochester's aristocratic indifference to commercial publishing has left his editors many vexing issues of authorship and of attribution. The evidence by which my editorial decisions have been guided is set out fully in the extensive notes to my larger Everyman edition. There too can be found more concrete information about the shadowy figures behind the proper names given to the targets of abuse and affection in Rochester's poetry, specific details of the literary and philosophic sources on which he drew, and extensive glossing of words whose usage has altered – or been abandoned – since the late seventeenth century.

To His Sacred Majesty

Virtue's triumphant shrine! Who dost engage
At once three kingdoms in a pilgrimage;
Which in ecstatic duty strive to come
Out of themselves as well as from their home:
Whilst England grows one camp, and London is   5
Itself the nation, not metropolis;
And loyal Kent renews her arts again,
Fencing her ways with moving groves of men;
Forgive this distant homage, which doth meet
Your blessed approach on sedentary feet: 10
And though my youth, not patient yet to bear
The weight of arms, denies me to appear
In steel before you, yet, Great Sir, approve
My manly wishes and more vigorous love;
In whom a cold respect were treason to   15
A father's ashes, greater then to you;
Whose one ambition 'tis for to be known
By daring loyalty
                              Your Wilmot's Son.

Impia blasphemi sileant concilia vulgi

Impia blasphemi sileant concilia vulgi:
    Absolvo medicos, innocuamque manum.
Curasset alios facili medicamine Morbos:
    Ulcera cum veniunt, Ars nihil ipsa valet.
Vultu fœmineo quævis vel pustula vulnus   5
    Lethale est, pulchras certior ense necat.
Mollia vel temeret si quando mitior ora,
    Evadat forsan femina, Diva nequat.
Cui par est Animæ Corpus, quæ tota venustas,
Formæ qui potis est, hæc superesse suæ?   10

JOHAN COMES ROFFEN. è Coll. Wadh.

To Her Sacred Majesty the Queen Mother

Respite, great Queen, your just and hasty fears,
There's no infection lodges in our tears.
Though our unhappy air be armed with death,
Yet sighs have an untainted guiltless breath.
Oh, stay awhile, and teach your equal skill   5
To understand and to support our ill.
You that in mighty wrongs an age have spent,
And seemed to have outlived even banishment:
Whom traitorous mischief sought its earliest prey,
When unto sacred blood it made its way;   10
And thereby did its black design impart,
To take his head, that wounded first his heart.
You that unmoved great Charles his ruin stood,
When three great nations sunk beneath the load:
Then a young daughter lost, yet balsam found   15
To staunch that new and freshly bleeding wound.
And after this, with fixed and steady eyes
Beheld your noble Gloucester's obsequies.
And then sustained the royal Princess' fall;
You only can lament her funeral.   20
But you will hence remove, and leave behind
Our sad complaints lost in the empty wind;
Those winds that bid you stay, and loudly roar
Destruction, and drive back unto the shore,
Shipwreck to safety, and the envy fly   25
Of sharing in this scene of tragedy.
Whilst sickness from whose rage you post away
Relents, and only now contrives your stay.
The lately fatal and infectious ill
Courts the fair Princess, and forgets to kill.   30
In vain on fevers curses we dispense,
And vent our passion's angry eloquence.
In vain we blast the ministers of Fate,
And the forlorn physicians imprecate;
Say they to death new poisons add, and fire;   35
Murder securely for reward and hire;
Art's basilisks, that kill whome'er they see,
And truly write Bills of Mortality;

Who, lest the bleeding corpse should them betray,
First drain those vital speaking streams away.   40
And will you by your flight take part with these?
Become yourself a third and new disease?
If they have caused our loss, then so have you,
Who take yourself and the fair Princess too:
For we, deprived, an equal damage have   45
When France doth ravish hence as when the grave.
     But that your choice the unkindness doth improve,
     And dereliction adds unto remove.

The Advice

All things submit themselves to your command,
Fair Celia, when it does not Love withstand;
The power it borrows from your eyes alone,
All but the god must yield to, who has none;
Were he not blind, such are the charms you have,   5
He'd quit his godhead to become your slave,
Be proud to act a mortal hero's part,
And throw himself for fame on his own dart.
But Fate has otherwise disposed of things,
In different bonds subjecting slaves and kings;   10
Fettered in forms of royal state are they,
While we enjoy the freedom to obey.
That Fate (like you resistless) does ordain
That Love alone should over beauty reign.
By harmony the universe does move,   15
And what is harmony, but mutual love?
See gentle brooks, how quietly they glide,
Kissing the rugged banks on either side,
Whilst in their crystal streams at once they show,
And with them feed the flowers which they bestow;   20
Though pressed upon by their too rude embrace,
In gentle murmurs they keep on their pace
To their loved sea; for even streams have desires:
Cool as they are, they feel Love's powerful fires;

And with such passion, that if any force   25
Stop or molest 'em in their amorous course,
They swell with rage, break down, and ravage o'er
The banks they kissed, the flowers they fed before.
Who would resist an empire so divine,
Which Universal Nature does enjoin?   30
Submit then, Celia, ere you be reduced;
For rebels vanquished once are vilely used.
And such are you, whene'er you dare obey
Another passion, and your love betray.
You are Love's citadel, by you he reigns,   35
And his proud empire o'er the world maintains;
He trusts you with his stratagems and arms,
His frowns, his smiles, and all his conquering charms.
Beauty's no more but the dead soil which Love
Manures, and does by wise commerce improve;   40
Sailing by sighs through seas of tears, he sends
Courtship from foreign hearts; for your own ends,
Cherish the trade; for as with Indians we
Get gold and jewels for our trumpery,
So to each other for their useless toys   45
Lovers afford whole magazines of joys:
But if you're fond of baubles, be, and starve,
Your geegaw reputation preserve;
Live upon modesty and empty fame,
Forgoing sense, for a fantastic name.   50

The Discovery

Celia, the faithful servant you disown
Would in obedience keep his love unknown;
But bright ideas such as you inspire,
We can no more conceal, than not admire.
My heart at home, in my own breast did dwell,   5
Like humble hermit in a peaceful cell,
Unknown, and undisturbed, it rested there,
Stranger alike to Hope, and to Despair.

But Love's tumultuous train does now invade
The sacred quiet of this hallowed shade;   10
His fatal flames shine out to every eye,
Like blazing comets in a winter's sky.
Fair and severe like heaven you enjoin
Commands that seem cross to your own design;
Forbidding what yourselves incline us to: 15
Since if from heavenly powers you will allow,
That all our faculties proceed, 'tis plain
Whate'er we will is what the Gods ordain.
But they and you, rights without limit have
Over your creatures, and (more yours) your slave: 20
And I am one, born only to admire,
Too humble e'er to hope, scarce to desire,
A thing whose bliss depends upon your will;
Who would be proud you'd deign to use him ill.
How can my passion merit your offence,   25
That challenges so little recompense?
Let me but ever love, and ever be
The example of your power and cruelty
Since so much scorn does in your breast reside,
Be more indulgent to its mother, Pride;   30
Kill all you strike, and trample on their graves,
But own the fates of your neglected slaves:
When in the crowd yours undistinguished lies,
You give away the triumph of your eyes:
Permit me then to glory in my chains,   35
My fruitless sighs, and my unpitied pains:
Perhaps obtaining this, you'll think I find
More mercy than your anger has designed;
But Love has carefully contrived for me
The last perfection of misery: 40
For to my state those hopes of common peace,
Which death affords to every wretch, must cease:
My worst of fates attends me in my grave,
Since, dying, I must be no more your slave.

Tunbridge Wells

At five this morning, when Phœbus raised his head
From Thetis' lap, I raised myself from bed;
And mounting steed, I trotted to the waters,
The rendezvous of fools, buffoons, and praters,
Cuckolds, whores, citizens, their wives and daughters.　5
My squeamish stomach I with wine had bribed
To undertake the dose it was prescribed.
But turning head, a cursed sudden crew
That innocent provision overthrew,
And without drinking made me purge and spew.　10
From coach-and-six a thing unwieldy rolled,
Whom lumber-cart more decently would hold;
As wise as calf it looked, as big as bully,
But handled proved a mere Sir Nicholas Cully:
A bawling fop, a natural Nokes, and yet　15
He dared to censure, as if he had wit:
To make him more ridiculous in spite,
Nature contrived the fool should be a knight.
How wise is Nature when she does dispense
A large estate to cover want of sense.　20
The man's a fool, 'tis true, but that's no matter,
For he's a mighty wit, with those that flatter;
But a poor blockhead is a wretched creature.
Though he alone was dismal sight enough,
His train contributed to set him off,　25
All of his shape, all of the self-same stuff:
No spleen, no malice need on them be thrown,
Nature has done the business of lampoon,
And in their looks their characters are shown.
Endeavouring this irksome sight to balk,　30
And a more irksome noise, their silly talk,
I silently slunk down to the Lower Walk:
But oft, when we would Charybdis shun,
Down upon Scylla 'tis our fate to run:
For here it was my cursed luck to find　35
As great a fop, though of another kind.
A tall, stiff fool, that walks in Spanish guise,
The buckram puppet never stirred his eyes,

But grave as owlet looked, as wood-cock wise.
He scorns the empty talk of this mad age,   40
And speaks all proverbs, sentences, adage;
Can with as great solemnity buy eggs
As a cabal can talk of their intrigues.
Master of ceremonies, yet can dispense
With the formality of talking sense.   45
From hence unto the Upper End I ran,
Where a new scene of foppery began.
A tribe of curates, priests, canonical elves,
Were company for none besides themselves.
They got together; each his distemper told,   50
Scurvy, stone, strangury; and some were bold
To charge the spleen to be their misery,
And on that wise disease bring infamy.
But none there were so modest to complain
Of want of learning, honesty, or brain,   55
The general disease of all that train:
These call themselves 'Ambassadors of Heaven',
Saucily pretending a commission given;
But should an Indian King, whose small command
Seldom extends t'above ten miles of land   60
Send forth such wretched fools on an embassage,
He'd find but small effect of such a message.
Listening I found the cob of all the rabble,
Was pert Bayes, with 'Importance Comfortable',
He being raised to an arch-deaconry,   65
By trampling on religious liberty,
Was grown so great, and looked so big and jolly,
Not being disturbed with care and melancholy,
Though Marvell has enough exposed his folly.
He drank to carry off some old remains   70
His lazy dull distemper left in 's veins:
Let him drink on, but 'tis not a whole flood
Can give sweetness to his blood,
Or make his nature or his manners good.
Importance drank too, though she'd been no sinner,   75
To wash away some dregs he had spewed in her.
Next after these, a fulsome Irish crew
Of silly Macs were offered to my view

The things did talk, but hearing what they said,
I did myself the kindness to evade: 80
Nature had placed these wretches below scorn,
They can't be called so vile as they were born.
Amidst the crowd next I myself conveyed,
For now there comes (whitewash and paint being laid)
Mother and daughter, mistress and the maid;   85
And squire with wig and pantaloons displayed.
But ne'er could conventicle, play, or fair
For a true medley with this herd compare.
Here lords, knights, squires, ladies, and countesses,
Chandlers, mum-bacon-women, sempstresses,   90
Were mixed together; nor did they agree
More in their humours than their quality.
Here waiting for gallant, young damsel stood,
Leaning on cane, and muffled up in hood;
The would-be wit, whose business 'twas to woo,   95
With hat removed, and solemn scrape of shoe,
Bowing advanceth, then genteelly shrugs,
And ruffled foretop he in order tugs,
And thus accosts her: 'Madam, methinks the weather
Is grown much more serene since you came hither: 100
You influence the heavens – and should the sun
Withdraw himself to see his rays outdone,
Your luminaries would supply the morn,
And make a day before the day be born.'
With mouth screwed up, and awkward winking eyes,   105
And breasts thrust forward – 'Lord, sir,' she replies,
'It is your goodness, and not my deserts
Which makes you show your learning, wit, and parts.'
He, puzzled, bites his nails, both to display
The sparkling ring, and think what next to say.   110
And thus breaks out afresh: 'Madam, egad,
Your luck last night at cards was mighty bad;
At cribbage, fifty-nine, and the next show
To make your game, and yet to want those two.
Gad damn me madam, I'm the son of a whore   115
If in my life I saw the likes before.'
To Peddlers' Hall he drags her soon, and says
The same dull stuff, a thousand different ways;

And then, more smartly to expound the riddle
Of all his prattle, gives her a Scotch fiddle. 120
Quite tired with this most dismal stuff I ran,
Where were two wives, and girl just fit for man;
Short was her breath, looks pale, and visage wan.
Some curtseys passed, and the old compliment
Of being glad to see each other spent, 125
With hand in hand they lovingly did walk,
And one began thus to renew the talk.
'I pray, good madam, if it may be thought
No rudeness, what cause was it hither brought
Your ladyship?' She soon replying, smiled, 130
'We have a good estate, but have no child;
And I'm informed these wells will make a barren
Woman as fruitful as a coney-warren.'
The first returned: 'For this cause I am come,
For I can have no quietness at home, 135
My husband grumbles, though we've gotten one,
This poor young girl, and mutters for a son;
And this, disturbed with headache-pangs and throws,
Is full sixteen, and yet had never *those*.'
She answered straight, 'Get her a husband, madam. 140
I married at that age, and never had 'em;
Was just like her; steel-waters let alone;
A back of steel will better bring 'em down.'
And ten-to-one but they themselves will try
The same way to increase their family. 145
Poor silly Fribble – who, by subtlety
Of midwife, truest friend to lechery,
Persuaded art to be at pains and charge,
To give thy wife occasion t'enlarge
Thy silly head! For here walk Cuff and Kick, 150
With brawny back and legs, and potent prick.
Who more substantially will cure thy wife,
And to her half-dead womb restore new life.
From these the waters got the reputation
Of good assistance unto generation. 155
Some warlike men were now got to the throng,
With hair tied back, singing a bawdy song.
Not much afraid, I got a nearer view,

And 'twas my chance to know the dreadful crew.
They were cadets, that seldom did appear,   160
Damned to the stint of thirty pounds a year;
With hawk on fist, or greyhound led in hand,
The dog and footboy sometimes do command;
But now, having trimmed a leash of spavined horse,
With three hard-pinched-for guineas in their purse.   165
Two rusty pistols, scarf about the arse,
Coat lined with red, they here presumed to swell:
This goes for captain, that for colonel.
Ev'n so the Bear-Garden ape, on his steed mounted,
No longer is a jackanapes accounted;   170
But is by virtue of his trumpery then
Called by the name of 'the young gentleman'.
Bless me, thought I, what thing is man that thus
In all his shapes he is ridiculous?
Ourselves with noise of reason we do please   175
In vain: humanity's our worst disease.
Thrice happy beasts are, who because they be
Of reason void, are so of foppery.

As Cloris full of harmless thought

As Cloris full of harmless thought
    Beneath the willows lay,
Kind love a comely shepherd brought
    To pass the time away.
She blushed to be encountered so,   5
    And chid the amorous swain;
But as she strove to rise and go
    He pulled her down again.

A sudden passion seized her heart
    In spite of her disdain,   10
She found a pulse in every part
    And love in every vein:
'Ah youth,' quoth she, 'what charms are these

That conquer and surprise?
Ah let me, for unless you please,   15
   I have no power to rise.'

She faintly spoke, and trembling lay,
   For fear he should comply,
But virgins' eyes their hearts betray,
   And give their tongues the lie;   20
Thus she who princes had denied,
   With all their pompous train,
Was in the lucky minute tried
   And yielded to a swain.

At last you'll force me to confess

At last you'll force me to confess
You need no arts to vanquish:
Such charms from nature you possess,
'Twere dullness not to languish;
Yet spare a heart you may surprise,   5
And give my tongue the glory
To scorn, while my unfaithful eyes
   Betray another story.

To a lady in a letter

Such perfect bliss, fair Cloris, we
   In our enjoyment prove,
'Tis pity restless jealousy
   Should mingle with our love.

Let us (since wit has taught us how)   5
   Raise pleasure to the top:

You rival bottle must allow,
    I'll suffer rival fop.

Think not in this that I design
    Treason against Love's charms,   10
When following the god of wine
    I leave my Cloris' arms.

Since you have that, for all your haste,
    At which I'll ne'er repine,
Will take his liquor off as fast   15
    As I can take off mine.

There's not a brisk insipid spark
    That flutters in the town
But with your wanton eyes you mark
    Him out to be your own.   20

Nor do you think it worth your care
    How empty and how dull
The heads of your admirers are –
    So that their cods be full.

All this you freely may confess,   25
    Yet we'd ne'er disagree,
For did you love your pleasure less
    You were no match for me.

Whilst I my pleasure to pursue
    Whole nights am taking in   30
The lusty juice of grapes, take you
    The juice of lusty men.

Against Constancy

Tell me no more of constancy,
   That frivolous pretence,
Of cold age, narrow jealousy,
   Disease, and want of sense.

Let duller fools on whom kind chance   5
   Some easy heart has thrown,
Despairing higher to advance,
   Be kind to one alone.

Old men and weak, whose idle flame
   Their own defects discovers,   10
Since changing can but spread their shame,
   Ought to be constant lovers.

But we, whose hearts do justly swell,
   With no vain-glorious pride,
Who know how we in love excel,   15
   Long to be often tried.

Then bring my bath, and strew my bed,
   As each kind night returns,
I'll change a mistress till I'm dead,
   And fate change me for worms.   20

While on those lovely looks I gaze

While on those lovely looks I gaze,
   To see a wretch pursuing,
In raptures of a blessed amaze
   His pleasing happy ruin:

'Tis not for pity that I move,   5
   His fate is too aspiring;
Whose heart broke with a load of love,
   Dies wishing and admiring.

But, if this murder you'd forgo,
    Your slave from death removing,   10
Let me your art of charming know,
    Or learn you mine of loving.

But whether life or death betide,
    In love, 'tis equal measure;
The victor lives with empty pride,   15
    The vanquished dies with pleasure.

My Lord All-Pride

Bursting with pride, the loathed impostume swells,
Prick him, he sheds his venom straight, and smells.
But 'tis so lewd a scribbler, that he writes,
With as much force to nature as he fights.
Hardened in shame, 'tis such a baffled fop   5
That every schoolboy whips him like a top.
And, with his arm and head, his brain's so weak
That his starved fancy is compelled to rake
Among the excrements of others' wit,
To make a stinking meal of what they shit.   10
So swine for nasty meat to dunghill run,
And toss their gruntling snouts up when they've done.
Against his stars the coxcomb ever strives,
And to be something they forbid, contrives:
With a red nose, splay foot, and goggle eye,   15
A ploughman's looby mien, face all awry,
With stinking breath, and every loathsome mark,
The Punchinello sets up for a spark.
With equal self-conceit too he bears arms,
But with that vile success his part performs   20
That he burlesques his trade; and what is best
In others turns, like Harlequin, to jest.
So have I seen at Smithfield's wondrous fair,

When all his brother monsters flourish there,
A lubbard elephant divert the town   25
With making legs, and shooting off a gun.
Go where he will, he never finds a friend,
Shame and derision all his steps attend.
Alike abroad, at home, i'th' camp, and Court,
This Knight o'th' Burning Pestle makes us sport.   30

A Letter fancied from Artemisa in the Town to Chloe in the Country

Chloe,
  In verse by your command I write;
Shortly you'll bid me ride astride, and fight.
These talents better with our sex agree,
Than lofty flights of dangerous poetry.
Amongst the men – I mean, the men of wit –   5
At least they passed for such, before they writ –
How many bold adventurers for the bays,
Proudly designing large returns of praise,
Who durst that stormy, pathless world explore,
Were soon tossed back, and wrecked on the dull shore,   10
Broke of that little stock they had before?
How would a woman's tottering bark be tossed,
Where stoutest ships – the men of wit – are lost?
When I reflect on this, I straight grow wise,
And my own self I gravely thus advise: 15
Dear Artemisa, poetry is a snare:
Bedlam has many mansions: have a care.
Your Muse diverts you, makes your reader sad;
You fancy you're inspired; he thinks you mad.
Consider too, 'twill be discreetly done,   20
To make yourself the fiddle of the town;
To find th' ill-humoured pleasure at their need,
Scorned if you fail, and cursed though you succeed.
Thus, like an arrant woman, as I am,

No sooner well-convinced writing's a shame,   25
That 'whore' is scarce a more reproachful name
Than 'poetess':
As men that marry, or as maids that woo.
'Cause 'tis the very worst thing they can do,
Pleased with the contradiction, and the sin,   30
Methinks I stand on thorns till I begin.
Y'expect at least to hear what loves have passed
In this lewd town, since you and I met last.
What change has happened, of intrigues, and whether
The old ones last, or who and who's together.   35
But how, my dearest Chloe, shall I set
My pen to write what I would fain forget?
Or name that lost thing (Love) without a tear,
Since so debauched by ill-customs here?
Love, the most generous passion of the mind,   40
The softest refuge innocence can find,
The safe director of unguided youth,
Fraught with kind wishes, and secured by truth,
That cordial drop heaven in our cup has thrown,
To make the nauseous draught of life go down,   45
On which one only blessing God might raise
In lands of atheists, subsidies of praise –
For none did ere so dull and stupid prove
But felt a god, and blessed his power in love –
This only joy, for which poor we were made,   50
Is grown like play, to be an arrant trade:
The rooks creep in, and it has got of late
As many little cheats and tricks as that.
But what yet more a woman's heart would vex,
'Tis chiefly carried on by our own sex,   55
Our silly sex, who born like monarchs, free,
Turn gypsies for a meaner liberty,
And hate restraint, though but from infamy.
They call whatever is not common 'nice',
And deaf to nature's rules, or love's advice,   60
Forsake the pleasures to pursue the vice.
To an exact perfection they have wrought
The action love, the passion is forgot.

'Tis below wit, they tell you, to admire,
And e'en without approving, they desire.   65
Their private wish obeys the public voice,
'Twixt good and bad, whimsy decides, not choice.
Fashions grow up for taste, at forms they strike:
They know what they would have, not what they like.
Bovey's a beauty, if some few agree   70
To call him so; the rest to that degree
Affected are, that with their ears they see.
Where I was visiting the other night,
Comes a fine lady with her humble knight,
Who had prevailed on her, by her own skill,   75
At his request, though much against his will,
To come to London.
As the coach stopped we heard her voice, more loud
Than a great-bellied woman in a crowd,
Telling the knight that her affairs require   80
He for some hours obsequiously retire.
I think she was ashamed to have him seen –
Hard fate of husbands – the gallant had been,
Though a diseased ill-favoured fool, brought in.
'Dispatch,' says she, 'your business you pretend,   85
That beastly visit to your drunken friend;
A bottle ever makes you look so fine!
Methinks I long to smell you stink of wine.
Your country-drinking breath's enough to kill –
Sour ale corrected with a lemon pill –   90
Prithee farewell. We'll meet again anon.'
The necessary thing bows, and is gone.
She flies upstairs, and all the haste does show
That fifty antic postures will allow,
And then bursts out – 'Dear madam, am not I   95
The alteredest creature breathing? Let me die,
I find myself ridiculously grown,
Embarrassée with being out of town,
Rude and untaught, like any Indian Queen;
My country nakedness is strangely seen.   100
How is love governed? Love that rules the State?
And pray, who are the men most worn of late?

When I was married, fools were *à la mode*,
The men of wit were then held *incommode*,
Slow of belief, and fickle in desire,   105
Who, ere they'll be persuaded, must inquire,
As if they came to spy, not to admire.
With searching wisdom, fatal to their ease,
They still find out why what may should not please;
Nay, take themselves for injured if we dare   110
Make 'em think better of us than we are;
And if we hide our frailties from their sights,
Call us deceitful jilts, and hypocrites.
They little guess, who at our arts are grieved,
The perfect joy of being well-deceived.   115
Inquisitive as jealous cuckolds grow,
Rather than not be knowing, they will know
What being known creates their certain woe.
Women should these of all mankind avoid,
For wonder by clear knowledge is destroyed.   120
Woman, who is an arrant bird of night,
Bold in the dusk, before a fool's dull sight
Should fly, when reason brings the glaring light;
But the kind easy fool, apt to admire
Himself, trusts us: his follies all conspire   125
To flatter his, and favour our desire.
Vain of his proper merit, he with ease
Believes we love him best, who best can please.
On him our common gross dull flatteries pass,
Ever most joyful when most made an ass.   130
Heavy to apprehend, though all mankind
Perceive us false, the fop concerned is blind,
Who doting on himself
Thinks everyone that sees him of his mind.
These are true women's men – ' Here, forced to cease   135
Through want of breath, not will to hold her peace,
She to the window runs, where she had spied
Her much esteemed dear friend the monkey, tied.
With forty smiles, as many antic bows
And if 't had been the lady of the house,   140
The dirty chattering monster she embraced,

And made it this fine tender speech at last:
'Kiss me, thou curious miniature of man.
How odd thou art! How pretty! How japan!
Oh I could live and die with thee – ' Then on,   145
For half an hour in compliment she ran.
I took this time to think what Nature meant,
When this mixed thing into the world she sent,
So very wise, yet so impertinent.
One who knew everything, who 'twas thought fit   150
Should be a fool through choice, not want of wit:
Whose foppery without the help of sense
Could ne'er have rise to such an excellence.
Nature's as lame in making a true fop
As a philosopher; the very top   155
And dignity of folly we attain
By curious search, and labour of the brain,
By observation, counsel, and deep thought.
God never made a coxcomb worth a groat;
We owe that name to industry and art.   160
An eminent fool must be a fool of parts,
And such a one was she, who had turned o'er
As many books as men, loved much, read more,
Had a discerning wit; to her was known
Everyone's fault and merit, but her own.   165
All the good qualities that ever blessed
A woman so distinguished from the rest,
Except discretion only, she possessed.
'But now, monsieur, dear Pug,' she cries, 'Adieu!'
And the discourse broke off does thus renew: 170
'You smile to see me, whom the world perchance
Mistakes to have some wit, so far advance
The interest of fools, that I approve
Their merit more than men of wit, in love.
But in our sex too many proofs there are   175
Of such whom wits undo, and fools repair.
This in my time was so observed a rule,
Hardly a wench in town but had her fool.
The meanest common slut, who long was grown
The jest and scorn of every pit-buffoon,   180
Had yet left charms enough to have subdued

Some fop or other, fond to be thought lewd.
Foster could make an Irish lord a Nokes,
And Betty Morris had her City-Cokes.
A woman's ne'er so ruined but she can   185
Be still revenged on her undoer, man.
How lost so e'er, she'll find some lover, more
A lewd abandoned fool than she's a whore.
That wretched thing Corinna, who had run
Through all the several ways of being undone,   190
Cozened at first by love, and living then
By turning the too-dear-bought trick on men:
Gay were the hours, and winged with joy they flew,
When first the town her early beauty knew;
Courted, admired, and loved, with presents fed,   195
Youth in her looks, and pleasure in her bed
Till fate, or her ill-angel, thought fit
To make her dote upon a man of wit,
Who found 'twas dull to love above a day,
Made his ill-natured jest, and went away.   200
Now scorned by all, forsaken and oppressed,
She's a *memento mori* to the rest.
Diseased, decayed, to take up half-a-crown
Must mortgage her long scarf and mantua gown.
Poor creature! Who, unheard of as a fly,   205
In some dark hole must all the winter lie,
And want and dirt endure a whole half-year,
That for one month she tawdry may appear.
In Easter Term she gets her a new gown,
When my young Master Worship comes to town,   210
From pedagogue and mother just set free,
The heir and hopes of a great family,
Which with strong ale and beef the country rules,
And ever since the Conquest have been fools.
And now with careful prospect to maintain   215
This character, lest crossing of the strain
Should mend the booby breed, his friends provide
A cousin of his own to be his bride;
And thus set out –
With an estate, no wit, and a young wife   220
(The solid comforts of a coxcomb's life),

Dunghill and pease forsook, he comes to town,
Turns spark, learns to be lewd, and is undone.
Nothing suits worse with vice than want of sense,
Fools are still wicked at their own expense.   225
This o'ergrown schoolboy lost Corinna wins,
And at first dash, to make an ass begins;
Pretends to like a man who has not known
The vanities nor vices of the town,
Fresh in his youth, and faithful in his love,   230
Eager of joys which he does seldom prove;
Healthful and strong, he does no pains endure
But what the fair one he adores can cure;
Grateful for favours, does the sex esteem,
And libels none for being kind to him.   235
Then of the lewdness of the times complains,
Rails at the wits and atheists, and maintains
'Tis better than good sense, than power or wealth,
To have a love untainted, youth, and health.
Th' unbred puppy, who had never seen   240
A creature look so gay, or talk so fine,
Believes, then falls in love, and then in debt,
Mortgages all, e'en to the ancient seat,
To buy his mistress a new house for life;
To give her plate and jewels, robs his wife;   245
And when to the height of fondness he is grown,
'Tis time to poison him, and all's her own.
Thus meeting in her common arms his fate,
He leaves her bastard heir to his estate;
And as the race of such an owl deserves,   250
His own dull lawful progeny he starves.
Nature, who never made a thing in vain,
But does each insect to some end ordain,
Wisely contrived kind keeping-fools, no doubt,
To patch up vices men of wit wear out.'   255
Thus she ran on two hours, some grains of sense
Still mixed with volleys of impertinence.
But now 'tis time I should some pity show
To Chloe, since I cannot choose but know
Readers must reap the dullness writers sow.   260
By the next post such stories I will tell

As joined with these shall to a volume swell,
As true as heaven, more infamous than hell.
But now you're tired, and so am I.

                                        Farewell.

A Very Heroical Epistle
in answer to Ephelia

Madam,
    If you're deceived, it is not by my cheat,
For all disguises are below the great.
What man or woman upon earth can say
I ever used 'em well above a day?
How is it then that I inconstant am?   5
He changes not who always is the same.
In my dear self I centre everything,
My servants, friends, my mistress and my king,
Nay, heaven and earth to that one point I bring.
Well-mannered, honest, generous and stout –   10
Names, by dull fools, to plague mankind found out.
Should I regard, I must myself constrain,
And 'tis my maxim to avoid all pain.
You fondly look for what none ere could find,
Deceive yourself, and then call me unkind;   15
And by false reasons would my falsehood prove;
For 'tis as natural to change, as love.
You may as justly at the sun repine
Because alike it does not always shine;
No glorious thing was ever made to stay,   20
My blazing star but visits, and away;
As fatal too it shines as those i' th' skies,
'Tis never seen but some great lady dies.
The boasted favour you so precious hold,
To me's no more than changing of my gold;   25
Whate'er you gave, I paid you back in bliss!
There where's the obligation, pray, of this?

If heretofore you found grace in my eyes,
Be thankful for it, and let that suffice.
But women, beggar-like, still haunt the door   30
Where they've received a charity before.
    Oh happy Sultan! Whom we barbarous call!
How much refined art thou above us all?
Who envies not the joys of thy serail?
Thee, like some god, the trembling crowd adore,   35
Each man's thy slave, and womankind, thy whore.
Methinks I see thee underneath the shade
Of golden canopies, supinely laid;
Thy crouching slaves, all silent as the night,
But at thy nod, all active as the light!   40
Secure in solid sloth, thou there dost reign,
And feel'st the joys of love, without the pain.
Each female courts thee with a wishing eye,
Whilst thou with awful pride, walk'st careless by,
Till thy kind pledge at last marks out the dame   45
Thou fanciest most to quench thy present flame:
Then from thy bed, submissive she retires,
And thankful for the grace, no more requires.
No loud reproach, nor fond unwelcome sound
Of women's tongues, thy sacred ear dares wound.   50
If any do, a nimble mute straight ties
The true-love-knot, and stops her foolish cries.
    Thou fear'st no injured kinsman's threatening blade,
Nor midnight ambushes, by rivals laid.
While where with aching heart, our joys we taste,   55
Disturbed by swords, like Damocles his feast.

Upon Nothing

Nothing, thou Elder Brother even to Shade,
Thou had'st a being ere the world was made,
And (well-fixed) art alone of ending not afraid.

Ere Time and Place were, Time and Place were not,
When Primitive Nothing something straight begot,   5
Then all proceeded from the great united – what?

Something, the general attribute of all,
Severed from thee, its sole original,
Into thy boundless self must undistinguished fall.

Yet something did thy mighty power command,   10
And from thy fruitful emptiness's hand
Snatched men, beasts, birds, fire, water, air, and land.

Matter, the wickedest offspring of thy race,
By Form assisted, flew from thy embrace,
And rebel light obscured thy reverend dusky face.   15

With Form and Matter, Time and Place did join,
Body, thy foe, with these did leagues combine,
To spoil thy peaceful realm and ruin all thy line.

But turncoat Time assists the foe in vain,
And bribed by thee, destroys their short-lived reign,   20
And to thy hungry womb drive back thy slaves again.

Though mysteries are barred from laic eyes,
And the Divine alone with warrant pries
Into thy bosom, where thy truth in private lies,

Yet this of thee the wise may truly say: 25
Thou from the virtuous, nothing dost delay,
And to be part of thee, the wicked wisely pray.

Great Negative, how vainly would the wise
Enquire, define, distinguish, teach, devise,
Didst thou not stand to point their blind philosophies.   30

Is or Is Not, the two great ends of Fate,
And True or False, the subject of debate
That perfect or destroy the vast designs of State –

When they have racked the politician's breast,
Within thy bosom most securely rest,   35
And when reduced to thee are least unsafe and blessed.

But (Nothing) why does Something still permit
That Sacred Monarchs should at Council sit
With persons highly thought, at best for nothing fit,

While weighty Something modestly abstains   40
From Princes' coffers and from Statesmen's brains,
And nothing there like stately Nothing reigns?

Nothing, who dwells with fools in grave disguise,
For whom they reverend shapes and forms devise,
Lawn-sleeves and furs and gowns, when they like thee look
     wise: 45

French Truth, Dutch Prowess, British Policy,
Hibernian Learning, Scotch Civility,
Spaniards' Dispatch, Danes' Wit, are mainly seen in thee;

The great man's gratitude to his best friend,
Kings' promises, whores' vows, towards thee they bend,   50
Flow swiftly into thee, and in thee ever end.

A Satire Against Mankind

Were I – who to my cost already am
One of those strange, prodigious creatures, man –
A spirit free to choose for my own share
What sort of flesh and blood I pleased to wear,
I'd be a dog, a monkey, or a bear,   5
Or anything but that vain animal,
Who is so proud of being rational.

His senses are too gross; and he'll contrive
A sixth, to contradict the other five;
And before certain instinct will prefer   10
Reason, which fifty times for one does err.
Reason, an *ignis fatuus* of the mind,
Which leaving light of nature, sense, behind,
Pathless and dangerous wand'ring ways it takes,
Through Error's fenny bogs and thorny brakes;   15
Whilst the misguided follower climbs with pain
Mountains of whimseys, heaped in his own brain;
Stumbling from thought to thought, falls headlong down,
Into Doubt's boundless sea where, like to drown,
Books bear him up awhile, and make him try   20
To swim with bladders of Philosophy;
In hopes still to o'ertake the escaping light;
The vapour dances, in his dazzling sight,
Till spent, it leaves him to eternal night.
Then old age and experience, hand in hand,   25
Lead him to death, make him to understand,
After a search so painful, and so long,
That all his life he has been in the wrong:
Huddled in dirt the reasoning engine lies,
Who was so proud, so witty, and so wise.   30
Pride drew him in, as cheats their bubbles catch,
And made him venture, to be made a wretch.
His wisdom did his happiness destroy,
Aiming to know that world he should enjoy;
And Wit was his vain, frivolous pretence   35
Of pleasing others, at his own expense.
For wits are treated just like common whores,
First they're enjoyed, and then kicked out of doors;
The pleasure past, a threatening doubt remains,
That frights th' enjoyer with succeeding pains: 40
Women and men of wit are dangerous tools,
And ever fatal to admiring fools.
Pleasure allures, and when the fops escape,
'Tis not that they're beloved, but fortunate,
And therefore what they fear, at heart they hate.   45
    But now, methinks some formal band and beard
Takes me to task; come on sir, I'm prepared:

Then by your favour, anything that's writ
Against this jibing, jingling knack called Wit
Likes me abundantly: but you take care   50
Upon this point not to be too severe.
Perhaps my Muse were fitter for this part,
For I profess, I can be very smart
On Wit, which I abhor with all my heart;
I long to lash it in some sharp essay,   55
But your grand indiscretion bids me stay,
And turns my tide of ink another way.
What rage forments in your degenerate mind,
To make you rail at reason, and mankind?
Blessed glorious man! To whom alone kind heaven   60
An everlasting soul hath freely given;
Whom his great maker took such care to make,
That from himself he did the image take;
And this fair frame in shining reason dressed,
To dignify his nature above beast.   65
Reason, by whose aspiring influence
We take a flight beyond material sense,
Dive into mysteries, then soaring pierce
The flaming limits of the universe,
Search heaven and hell, find out what's acted there,   70
And give the world true grounds of hope and fear.
Hold might man, I cry, all this we know,
From the pathetic pen of Ingelo;
From Patrick's *Pilgrim*, Sibbes' *Soliloquies*,
And 'tis this very Reason I despise,   75
This supernatural gift that makes a mite
Think he's an image of the infinite;
Comparing his short life, void of all rest,
To the eternal, and the ever-blessed.
This busy, pushing stirrer-up of doubt,   80
That frames deep mysteries, then finds them out;
Filling with frantic crowds of thinking fools
The reverend bedlams, colleges and schools;
Borne on whose wings each heavy sot can pierce
The limits of the boundless universe: 85
So charming ointments make an old witch fly,
And bear a crippled carcass through the sky.

'Tis the exalted power whose business lies
In nonsense, and impossibilities.
This made a whimsical philosopher   90
Before the spacious world his tub prefer,
And we have modern cloistered coxcombs, who
Retire to think 'cause they have nought to do.
But thoughts are given for action's government;
Where action ceases, thought's impertinent: 95
Our sphere of action is life's happiness,
And he that thinks beyond thinks like an ass.
Thus, whilst against false reasoning I inveigh,
I own right reason, which I would obey:
That reason which distinguishes by sense,   100
And gives us rules of good and ill from thence;
That bounds desires, with a reforming will
To keep 'em more in vigour, not to kill.
Your reason hinders, mine helps to enjoy,
Renewing appetites yours would destroy.   105
My reason is my friend, yours is a cheat,
Hunger calls out, my reason bids me eat;
Perversely, yours your appetite does mock:
This asks for food, that answers, 'what's o'clock?'
     This plain distinction, sir, your doubt secures, 110
'Tis not true reason I despise, but yours.
Thus I think reason righted, but for man,
I'll ne'er recant, defend him if you can.
For all his pride, and his philosophy,
'Tis evident: beasts are in their own degree   115
As wise at least, and better far than he.
Those creatures are the wisest who attain,
By surest means, the ends at which they aim.
If therefore Jowler finds and kills the hares,
Better than Meres supplies committee chairs;   120
Though one's a statesman, th' other but a hound,
Jowler in justice would be wiser found.
You see how far man's wisdom here extends,
Look next if human nature makes amends;
Whose principles are most generous and just,   125
And to whose morals you would sooner trust:
Be judge yourself, I'll bring it to the test,

Which is the basest creature, man or beast?
Birds feed on birds, beasts on each other prey,
But savage man alone does man betray: 130
Pressed by necessity, they kill for food,
Man undoes man, to do himself no good.
With teeth and claws, by nature armed, they hunt
Nature's allowance, to supply their want.
But man, with smiles, embraces, friendships, praise,   135
Inhumanely his fellow's life betrays;
With voluntary pains works his distress,
Not through necessity, but wantonness.
For hunger or for love they bite, or tear,
Whilst wretched man is still in arms for fear.   140
For fear he arms, and is of arms afraid:
From fear, to fear, successively betrayed.
Base fear, the source whence his best passions came,
His boasted honour, and his dear-bought fame.
The lust of power, to whom he's such a slave,   145
And for the which alone he dares be brave;
To which his various projects are designed,
Which makes him generous, affable, and kind.
For which he takes such pains to be thought wise,
And screws his actions, in a forced disguise;   150
Leads a most tedious life in misery,
Under laborious, mean hypocrisy.
Look to the bottom of his vast design,
Wherein man's wisdom, power, and glory join:
The good he acts, the ill he does endure,   155
'Tis all from fear, to make himself secure.
Merely for safety after fame they thirst,
For all men would be cowards if they durst.
And honesty's against all common sense,
Men must be knaves, 'tis in their own defence.   160
Mankind's dishonest: if you think it fair
Among known cheats to play upon the square,
You'll be undone.
Nor can weak truth your reputation save,
The knaves will all agree to call you knave.   165
Wronged shall he live, insulted o'er, oppressed,

Who dares be less a villain than the rest.
Thus sir, you see what human nature craves,
Most men are cowards, all men should be knaves;
The difference lies, as far as I can see,   170
Not in the thing itself, but the degree;
And all the subject matter of debate
Is only, who's a knave of the first rate?

Addition

All this with indignation have I hurled
At the pretending part of the proud world,
Who, swollen with selfish vanity, devise,
False freedoms, holy cheats, and formal lies,
Over their fellow-slaves to tyrannise.   5
But if in Court so just a man there be,
(In Court, a just man – yet unknown to me)
Who does his needful flattery direct
Not to oppress and ruin, but protect;
Since flattery, which way soever laid,   10
Is still a tax on that unhappy trade.
If so upright a statesman you can find,
Whose passions bend to his unbiased mind,
Who does his arts and policies apply
To raise his country, not his family;   15
Nor while his pride owned avarice withstands,
Receives close bribes, from friends corrupted hands.
   Is there a churchman who on God relies?
Whose life, his faith and doctrine justifies?
Not one blown up, with vain prelatic pride,   20
Who for reproofs of sins does man deride;
Whose envious heart makes preaching a pretence
With his obstreperous, saucy eloquence,
To chide at kings, and rail at men of sense;
Who from his pulpit vents more peevish lies,   25
More bitter railings, scandals, calumnies,
Than at a gossiping are thrown about

When the good wives get drunk, and then fall out.
None of that sensual tribe, whose talents lie
In avarice, pride, sloth, and gluttony.   30
Who hunt good livings, but abhor good lives,
Whose lust exalted, to that height arrives,
They act adultery with their own wives.
And ere a score of years completed be,
Can from the loftiest pulpit proudly see,   35
Half a large parish their own progeny.
Nor doting bishop, who would be adored
For domineering at the Council board;
A greater fop, in business at fourscore,
Fonder of serious toys, affected more,   40
Than the gay, glittering fool at twenty proves,
With all his noise, his tawdry clothes and loves.
    But a meek, humble man, of honest sense,
Who preaching peace does practise continence;
Whose pious life's a proof he does believe   45
Mysterious truths which no man can conceive.
If upon Earth there dwell such god-like men,
I'll here recant my paradox to them,
Adores those shrines of virtue, homage pay,
And with the rabble world their laws obey.   50
If such there are, yet grant me this at least,
Man differs more from man than man from beast.

Translation: from Seneca's *Troades*

After death nothing is, and nothing, death;
The utmost limit of a gasp of breath.
Let the ambitious zealot lay aside
His hopes of heaven, whose faith is but his pride;
    Let slavish souls lay by their fear,   5
    Nor be concerned which way nor where
    After this life they shall be hurled.
Dead we become the lumber of the world,
And to that mass of matter shall be swept

Where things destroyed with things unborn are kept. 10
   Devouring time swallows us whole;
   Impartial death confounds body and soul.
For Hell and the foul fiend that rules
   God's everlasting fiery jails
   (Devised by rogues, dreaded by fools). 15
With his grim, grisly dog that keeps the door,
   Are senseless stories, idle tales.
   Dreams, whimseys, and no more.

On Mistress Willis

Against the charms our bollocks have
   How weak all human skill is!
Since they can make a man a slave
   To such a bitch as Willis.

Whom that I may describe throughout, 5
   Assist me bawdy powers:
I'll write upon a double clout,
   And dip my pen in flowers.

Her look's demurely impudent,
   Ungainly beautiful, 10
Her modesty is insolent,
   Her mirth is pert and dull.

A prostitute of all the town,
   And yet with no man friends,
She rails and scolds when she lies down, 15
   And curses when she spends.

Bawdy in thoughts, precise in words,
   Ill-natured, and a whore,
Her belly is a bag of turds,
   And her cunt's a common shore. 20

Love and Life

All my past life is mine no more,
   The flying hours are gone,
Like transitory dreams given o'er,
Whose images are kept in store
   By memory alone.   5

What ever is to come is not,
   How can it then be mine?
The present moment's all my lot,
And that as fast as it is got,
   Phyllis, is wholly thine.   10

Then talk not of inconstancy,
   False hearts, and broken vows,
If I, by miracle, can be,
This live-long minute true to thee,
   'Tis all that heaven allows.   15

The Disabled Debauchee

As some brave admiral, in former war,
Deprived of force, but pressed with courage still,
Two rival fleets appearing from afar,
Crawls to the top of an adjacent hill;

From whence (with thoughts full of concern) he views   5
The wise and daring conduct of the fight,
And each bold action to his mind renews
His present glory, and his past delight;

From his fierce eyes, flashes of rage he throws,
As from black clouds when lightning breaks away,   10
Transported, thinks himself amidst his foes,
And absent yet enjoys the bloody day;

So when my days of impotence approach,
And I'm by pox and wine's unlucky chance,
Driven from the pleasing billows of debauch,   15
On the dull shore of lazy temperance,

My pains at last some respite shall afford,
Whilst I behold the battles you maintain,
When fleets of glasses sail about the board,
From whose broadsides volleys of wit shall rain.   20

Nor shall the sight of honourable scars,
Which my too-forward valour did procure,
Frighten new-listed soldiers from the wars.
Past joys have more than paid what I endure.

Should hopeful youths (worth being drunk) prove nice,   25
And from their fair inviters meanly shrink,
'Twould please the ghost of my departed vice,
If at my counsel they repent and drink.

Or should some cold-complexioned sot forbid,
With his dull morals, our night's brisk alarms,   30
I'll fire his blood by telling what I did,
When I was strong and able to bear arms.

I'll tell of whores attacked, their lords at home,
Bawds' quarters beaten up, and fortress won,
Windows demolished, watches overcome,   35
And handsome ills by my contrivance done.

Nor shall our love-fits, Cloris, be forgot,
When each the well-looked link-boy strove t'enjoy,
And the best kiss was the deciding lot:
Whether the boy fucked you, or I the boy.   40

With tales like these I will such heat inspire,
As to important mischief shall incline.
I'll make them long some ancient church to fire,
And fear no lewdness they're called to by wine.

Thus statesman-like, I'll saucily impose,   45
And safe from danger valiantly advise,
Sheltered in impotence, urge you to blows,
And being good for nothing else, be wise.

By all love's soft, yet mighty powers

By all love's soft, yet mighty powers,
    It is a thing unfit,
That men should fuck in time of flowers,
    Or when the smock's beshit.

Fair nasty nymph, be clean and kind,   5
    And all my joys restore;
By using paper still behind,
    And sponges for before.

My spotless flames can ne'er decay,
    If after every close,   10
My smoking prick escape the fray,
    Without a bloody nose.

If thou would have me true, be wise,
    And take to cleanly sinning,
None but fresh lovers' pricks can rise,   15
    At Phyllis in foul linen.

On Poet Ninny

Crushed by that just contempt his follies bring
On his crazed head, the vermin fain would sting;
But never satire did so softly bite,
Or gentle George himself more gently write.
Born to no other but thy own disgrace,   5

Thou art a thing so wretched and so base
Thou canst not e'en offend, but with thy face:
And dost at once a sad example prove,
Of harmless malice, and of hopeless love.
All pride and ugliness! Oh how we loath   10
A nauseous creature so composed of both!
How oft have we thy capering person seen,
With dismal look, and melancholy mien?
The just reverse of Nokes, when he would be
Some mighty hero, and make love, like thee.   15
Thou art below being laughed at, out of spite,
Men gaze upon thee as a hideous sight
And cry, 'There goes the melancholy knight!'
There are some modish fools we daily see,
Modest and dull: why they are wits to thee!   20
For of all folly, sure the very top
Is a conceited ninny and a fop.
With face of farce joined to a head romancy
There's no such coxcomb as your fool of fancy.
But 'tis too much, on so despised a theme;   25
No man would dabble in a dirty stream;
The worst that I could write would be no more
Than what thy very friends have said before.

An Epistolary Essay
from M. G. to O. B.
upon their mutual poems

Dear friend,
   I hear this Town does so abound
With saucy censures, that faults are found
With what of late we (in poetic rage)
Bestowing, threw away on the dull age;
But howsoe'er envy their spleen may raise,   5
To rob my brow of the deserved bays,
Their thanks at least I merit since through me

They are partakers of your poetry;
And this is all I'll say in my defence,
T'obtain one line of your well-worded sense   10
I'd be content t'have writ *The British Prince*.
I'm none of those who think themselves inspired,
Nor write with the vain hopes to be admired;
But from a rule I have upon long trial,
T'avoid with care all sorts of self-denial.   15
Which way soe'er desire and fancy lead,
Contemning fame that path I boldly tread;
And if exposing what I take for wit
To my dear self a pleasure I beget
No matter though the censuring critics fret.   20
Those whom my Muse displeases are at strife
With equal spleen against my course of life,
The least delight of which I'd not forgo,
For all the flattering praise man can bestow.
If I designed to please, the way were then,   25
To mend my manners, rather than my pen;
The first's unnatural, therefore unfit,
And for the second, I despair of it,
Since grace is not so hard to get as wit.
Perhaps ill verses ought to be confined,   30
In mere good breeding, like unsavoury wind;
Were reading forced, I should be apt to think
Men might no more write scurvily than stink;
But 'tis your choice whether you'll read or no,
If likewise of your smelling it were so,   35
I'd fart just as I write, for my own ease,
Nor should you be concerned, unless you please:
I'll own that you write better than I do,
But I have as much need to write as you.
What though the excrement of my dull brain   40
Runs in a harsh, insipid strain,
Whilst your rich head eases itself of wit?
Must none but civet-cats have leave to shit?
In all I write, should sense, and wit, and rhyme
Fail me at once, yet something so sublime   45
Shall stamp my poem, that the world may see
It could have been produced by none but me.

And that's my end, for man can wish no more,
Than so to write, as none e'er writ before.
Yet why am I no poet of the times?   50
I have allusions, similes and rhymes,
And wit, or else 'tis hard that I alone
Of the whole race of mankind should have none.
Unequally, the partial hand of heaven
Has all but this one only blessing given: 55
The world appears like a great family,
Whose lord oppressed with pride and poverty,
(That to a few, great bounty he may show)
Is fain to starve the numerous train below;
Just so seems Providence, as poor, and vain,   60
Keeping more creatures than it can maintain.
Here 'tis profuse, and there it meanly saves,
And for one prince, it makes ten thousand slaves:
In wit alone 't had been magnificent,
Of which so just a share to each is sent   65
That the most avaricious are content.
For none e'er thought (the due division's such),
His own too little, or his friends' too much.
Yet most men show or find great want of wit,
Writing themselves, or judging what is writ: 70
But I, whom am of sprightly vigour full,
Look on mankind as envious and dull.
Born to myself, myself I like alone,
And must conclude my judgment good, or none.
For should my sense be nought, how could I know,   75
Whether another man's were good, or no?
Thus I resolve of my own poetry
That 'tis the best, and there's a fame for me.
If then I'm happy, what does it advance,
Whether to merit due, or arrogance?   80
Oh! But the world shall suffer for 't, not I.
Did e'er this saucy world and I agree
To let it have its beastly will on me?
Why should my prostituted sense be drawn
To every rule their musty customs spawn?   85
But men will censure you; 'tis two to one
Whene'er they censure, they'll be in the wrong.

There's not a thing on earth that I can name
So foolish, and so false, as common fame.
It calls the courtier knave, the plain man rude,   90
Haughty the grave, and the delightful lewd,
Impertinent the brisk, morose the sad,
Mean the familiar, the reserved one mad.
Poor helpless woman is not favoured more;
She's a sly hypocrite, or public whore.   95
Then who the devil would give this – to be free
From th' innocent reproach of infamy?
These things considered make me (in despite
Of idle rumour) keep at home and write.

Fair Cloris in a pigsty lay

Fair Cloris in a pigsty lay,
    Her tender herd lay by her.
She slept; in murmuring gruntlings they,
Complaining of the scorching day,
    Her slumbers thus inspire.   5

She dreamed while she with careful pains
    Her snowy arms employed
In ivory pails to fill out grains
One of her love-convicted swains
    Thus hasting to her, cried.   10

'Fly nymph, oh fly, ere 'tis too late
    A dear-loved life to save,
Rescue your bosom pig from Fate
Who now expires, hung in the gate
    That leads to Flora's cave.   15

'Myself had tried to set him free
    Rather than brought the news
But I am so abhorred by thee
That even thy darling's life from me
    I know thou wouldst refuse.'   20

Struck with the news as quick she flies
    As blushes to her face
Not the bright lightning from the skies
Nor love shot from her brighter eyes
    Move half so swift a pace.   25

This plot it seems the lustful slave
    Had laid against her honour,
Which not one god took care to save,
For he pursues her to the cave
    And throws himself upon her.   30

Now pierced is her virgin zone
    She feels the foe within it,
She hears a broken amorous groan,
The panting lover's fainting moan
    Just in the happy minute.   35

Frighted she wakes, and waking frigs.
    Nature thus kindly eased.
In dreams raised by her murmuring pigs,
And by her own thumb between her legs,
    She's innocent and pleased.   40

Actus Primus: Scena Prima

The Scene: a bed-chamber
Enter TARSANDER *and* SWIVEANTHE

TARSANDER: For standing tarses we kind Nature thank,
                  And yet adore those cunts that make 'em lank.
                  Unhappy mortals! Whose sublimest joy
                  Preys on itself, and does itself destroy.

SWIVEANTHE: Do not thy tarse, Nature's best gift, despise,   5
That cunt that made it fall will make it rise;
Though it awhile the amorous combat shun,
And seems from mine into thy belly run,
Yet 'twill return more vigorous, and more fierce
Than flaming drunkard, when he's dyed in
    tierce.   10
It but retires as losing gamesters do,
Till they have raised a stake to play anew.

TARSANDER: What pleasure has a gamester, if he knows
Whene'er he play that he must always lose?

SWIVEANTHE: What Pego loses, 'twere a pain to keep: 15
We say not that our nights are lost in sleep;
What pleasures we in those soft wars employ
We do not waste, but to the full enjoy.

                        Exit TARSANDER

                 Enter CELIA

CELIA: Madam, methinks those sleepy eyes declare
Too lately you have eased a lover's care.   20
I fear you have with interest repaid
Those eager thrusts which at your cunt he made.

SWIVEANTHE: With force united my soft heart he stormed,
Like age he doted, but like youth performed.
She that alone her lover can withstand   25
Is more than woman, or he less than man.

                        Exeunt

Give me leave to rail at you

Give me leave to rail at you,
I ask nothing but my due;
To call you false, and then to say,
You shall not keep my heart a day.

But (alas) against my will,   5
I must be your captive still.
Ah! be kinder then, for I,
Cannot change, and would not die.

Kindness has resistless charms,
All besides but weakly move,   10
Fiercest anger it disarms,
And clips the wings of flying love.
Beauty does the heart invade,
Kindness only can persuade;
It gilds the lover's servile chain   15
And makes the slave grow pleased and vain.

The Answer

Nothing adds to your fond fire,
More than scorn and cold disdain,
I to cherish your desire,
Kindness used but 'twas in vain.
You insulted on your slave,   5
Humble love you soon refused.
Hope not then a power to have
Which ingloriously you used.

Think not, Thyrsis, I will e'er
By my love my empire lose,   10
You grow constant through despair,
Love returned you would abuse.
Though you still possess my heart,
Scorn and rigour I must feign.
Ah, forgive that only art,   15
Love has left your love to gain.

You that could my heart subdue
To new conquests, ne'er pretend,
Let your example make me true,

And of a conquered foe, a friend.   20
Then if e'er I should complain,
Of your empire, or my chain,
Summon all your powerful charms,
And fell the rebel in your arms.

To all curious critics and admirers of metre

Have you seen the raging stormy main
Toss a ship up, then cast her down again?
Sometimes she seems to touch the very skies,
And then again upon the sand she lies.
Or have you seen a bull, when he is jealous,   5
How he does tear the ground, and roars and bellows?
Or have you seen the pretty turtle-dove,
When she laments the absence of her love?
Or have you seen the fairies, when they sing
And dance with mirth together in a ring?   10
Or have you seen our gallants make a pudder,
With Fair and Grace, and Grace and Fair Anne Strudder?
Or have you seen the daughters of Apollo
Pour down their rhyming liquors in a hollow cane?
In spongy brain, congealing into verse?   15
If you have seen all this – then kiss mine arse.

The Fall

How blessed was the created state
    Of Man and Woman, ere they fell,
Compared to our unhappy state!
    We need not fear another hell:

Naked beneath cool shades they lay,   5
    Enjoyment waited on desire;

Each member did their wills obey:
    Nor could a wish set pleasure higher.

But we, poor slaves to hope and fear,
    Are never of our joys secure: 10
They lessen still, as they draw near,
    And none but dull delights endure.

Then, Cloris, while I duty pay,
    The nobler tribute of a heart;
Be not you so severe to say   15
    You love me for a frailer part.

Régime de Vivre

I rise at eleven, I dine about two,
I get drunk before seven, and the next thing I do,
I send for my whore, when for fear of a clap,
I spend in her hand, and I spew in her lap;
Then we quarrel and scold, till I fall fast asleep,   5
When the bitch growing bold, to my pocket does creep.
Then slyly she leaves me, and to revenge the affront,
At once she bereaves me of money and cunt.
If by chance then I wake, hot-headed and drunk,
What a coil do I make for the loss of my punk!   10
I storm, and I roar, and I fall in a rage.
And missing my whore, I bugger my page.
Then crop-sick all morning I rail at my men,
And in bed I lie yawning till eleven again.

The Mock Song

I swive as well as others do,
    I'm young, not yet deformed,
My tender heart, sincere and true,
    Deserved not to be scorned.
Why Phyllis then, why will you swive   5
    With forty lovers more?
Can I (said she) with nature strive,
    Alas I am, alas I am a whore.

Were all my body larded o'er,
    With darts of love, so thick,   10
That you might find in every pore,
    A well-stuck, standing prick:
Whilst yet my eyes alone were free,
    My heart would never doubt,
In amorous rage, and ecstasy,   15
    To wish those eyes, to wish those eyes fucked out.

On Rome's Pardons

If Rome can parson sin, as Romans hold,
And if those pardons can be bought and sold,
It were no sin t'adore, and worship gold.

If they can purchase pardons with a sum,
For sins they may commit in time to come,   5
And for sins past, 'tis very well for Rome.

At this rate they are happiest that have most,
They'll purchase heaven at their own proper cost,
Alas the poor! All that are so are lost.

Whence came this knack, or whence did it begin?   10
What author have they, or who brought it in?
Did Christ e'er keep a custom-house for sin?

Some subtle devil, without more ado,
Did certainly this sly invention brew,
To gull 'em of their souls and money too.   15

In the Fields of Lincoln's Inn

In the Fields of Lincolns Inn
Underneath a tattered blanket,
On a flock-bed, God be thanked,
Feats of active love were seen.

Phyllis, who you know loves swiving,   5
As the Gods love pious prayers,
Lay most pensively contriving,
How to fuck with pricks by pairs.

Coridon's aspiring tarse,
Which to cunt had ne'er submitted,   10
Wet with amorous kiss she fitted
To her less-frequented arse.

Strephon's was a handful longer,
Stiffly propped with eager lust;
None for champion was more stronger,   15
This into her cunt he thrust.

Now for Civil Wars prepare,
Raised by fierce intestine bustle,
When these heroes meeting jostle,
In the bowels of the fair.   20

They tilt, and thrust with horrid pudder,
Blood and slaughter is decreed;
Hurling souls at one another,
Wrapped in flakey clots of seed.

Nature had 'twixt cunt and arse   25
Wisely placed firm separation;

God knows else what desolation
Had ensured from warring tarse.

Though Fate a dismal end did threaten,
It proved no worse than was desired: 30
The nymph was sorely bollock-beaten,
Both the shepherds soundly tired.

Love a woman! Y'are an ass!

Love a woman! Y'are an ass!
  'Tis a most insipid passion
To choose out for your happiness
  The idlest part of God's creation.

Let the porter and the groom,   5
  Things designed for dirty slaves,
Drudge in fair Aurelia's womb,
  To get supplies for age, and graves.

Farewell woman, I intend,
  Henceforth every night to sit,   10
With my lewd well-natured friend,
  Drinking to engender wit.

Then give me health, wealth, mirth, and wine,
  And if busy love entrenches,
There's a sweet soft page, of mine,   15
  Does the trick worth forty wenches.

Woman's Honour

Love bade me hope, and I obeyed,
Phyllis continued still unkind,
'Then you may e'en despair,' he said,
'In vain I strive to change her mind.

'Honour's got in, and keeps her heart;   5
Durst he but venture once abroad
In my own right I'd take your part,
And show myself the mightier god.'

This huffing Honour domineers
In breasts alone where he has place;   10
But if true generous Love appears,
The hector dares not show his face.

Let me still languish and complain,
Be most unhumanly denied,
I have some pleasure in my pain,   15
She can have none with all her pride.

I fall a sacrifice to Love;
She lives a wretch for Honour's sake;
Whose tyrant does most cruel prove,
The difference is not hard to make.   20

Consider real honour then,
You'll find hers cannot be the same,
'Tis noble confidence in men,
In women, mean mistrustful shame.

A Ramble in St James's Park

Much wine had passed, with grave discourse
Of who fucks who, and who does worse,
Such as you usually do hear
From them that diet at *The Bear*.
When I, who still take care to see   5
Drunkenness relieved by lechery,
Went out into St James's Park,
To cool my head, and fire my heart.
But though St James has the honour on't,
'Tis consecrate to prick and cunt.   10
There, by a most incestuous birth,
Strange woods spring from the teeming earth:
For they relate how heretofore,
When ancient Pict began to whore,
Deluded of his assignation   15
(Jilting, it seems, was then in fashion)
Poor pensive lover, in this place
Would frig upon his mother's face;
Whence rows of mandrakes tall did rise,
Whose lewd tops fucked the very skies.   20
Each imitative branch does twine
In some love fold of Arentine;
And nightly now beneath their shade
Are buggeries, rapes, and incests made:
Unto this all-sin-sheltering grove   25
Whores of the bulk and the alcove,
Great ladies, chamber-maids, and drudges,
The rag-picker and heiress trudges;
Car-men, divines, great lords, and tailors,
Prentices, pimps, poets, and jailers,   30
Footmen, fine fops, do here arrive,
And here promiscuously they swive.
   Along these hallowed walks it was
That I beheld Corinna pass.
Whoever had been by to see   35
The proud disdain she cast on me,
Through charming eyes he would have swore
She dropped from heaven that very hour,

Forsaking the divine abode
In scorn of some despairing god.   40
But mark what creatures women are,
So infinitely vile and fair:
Three knights o'th' elbow and the slur
With wriggling tails made up to her.

    The first was of your Whitehall blades,   45
Near kin to the Mother of the Maids,
Graced by whose favour he was able
To bring a friend to the Waiters' table,
Where he had heard Sir Edward Sutton
Say how the King loved Banstead mutton;   50
Since when he'd ne'er be brought to eat,
By 's goodwill, any other meat.
In this, as well as all the rest,
He ventures to do like the best;
But wanting common sense, th' ingredient   55
In choosing well not least expedient,
Converts abortive imitation
To universal affectation.
So he not only eats and talks,
But feels and smells, sits down and walks,   60
Nay, looks, and lives, and loves by rote,
In an old tawdry birthday coat.

    The second was a Grays Inn wit,
A great inhabiter of the Pit,
Where critic-like he sits and squints,   65
Steals pocket handkerchiefs and hints
From 's neighbour and the comedy,
To court and pay his landlady.

    The third, a lady's eldest son
Within few years of twenty-one,   70
Who hopes from his propitious fate,
Against he comes to his estate,
By these two worthies to be made
A most accomplished, tearing blade.

    One in a strain 'twixt tune and nonsense   75
Cries, 'Madam, I have loved you long since.
Permit me your fair hand to kiss.'
When at her mouth her cunt says, 'Yes.'

In short, without much more ado,
Joyful and pleased, away she flew,   80
And with these three confounded asses,
From Park to hackney-coach she passes.
   So a proud bitch does lead about
Of humble curs the amorous rout,
Who most obsequiously do hunt   85
The savoury scent of salt-swollen cunt.
Some power more patient now relate
The sense of this surprising fate.
Gods! That a thing admired by me
Should fall to so much infamy!   90
Had she picked out to rub her arse on
Some stiff-pricked clown, or well-hung parson,
Each job of whose spermatic sluice
Had filled her cunt with wholesome juice,
I the proceeding should have praised   95
In hope she had quenched a fire I raised.
Such natural freedoms are but just,
There's something generous in mere lust.
But to turn damned abandoned jade,
When neither head nor tail persuade,   100
To be a whore in understanding,
A passive pot for fools to spend in!
The devil played booty sure with thee
To bring a blot of infamy.
But why am I, of all mankind,   105
To so severe a fate designed?
Ungrateful! Why this treachery
To humble, fond, believing me?
Who gave you privileges above
The nice allowances of love?   110
Did ever I refuse to bear
The meanest part your lust could spare?
When your lewd cunt came spewing home,
Drenched with the seed of half the town,
My dram of sperm was supped up after   115
For the digestive surfeit-water.
Full-gorged at another time
With a vast meal of nasty slime,

Which your devouring cunt had drawn
From porters' backs and footmen's brawn,   120
I was content to serve you up
My bollocks-full for your grace-cup.
Nor ever thought it an abuse
While you had pleasure for excuse.
You that could make my heart away   125
For noise and colours, and betray
The secrets of my tender hours
To such knight-errant paramours.
When leaning on your faithless breast,
Wrapped in security and rest,   130
Soft kindness all my powers did move,
And reason lay dissolved in love.

     May stinking vapour choke your womb,
Such as the men you dote upon.
May your depraved appetite,   135
That could in whiffling fools delight,
Beget such frenzies in your mind
You may go mad for the North wind;
And fixing all your hopes upon't,
To have him bluster in your cunt,   140
Turn up your longing arse to the air,
And perish in a wild despair.

     But cowards shall forget to rant,
Schoolboys to frig, old whores to paint;
The Jesuits fraternity   145
Shall leave the use of buggery;
Crab-louse, inspired with grace divine,
From earthly cod to heaven shall climb;
Physicians shall believe in Jesus,
And disobedience cease to please us,   150
Ere I desist with all my power
To plague this woman and undo her.
But my revenge will best be timed
When she is married, that is: limed.
In that most lamentable state   155
I'll make her feel my scorn and hate.
Pelt her with scandals, truth or lies,
And her poor cur with jealousies,

Till I have torn him from her breech,
While she whines like a dog-drawn bitch,   160
Loathed and despised, kicked out of town,
Into some dirty hole alone,
To chew the cud of misery,
And know she owes it all to me.
    And may no woman better thrive   165
    That dares profane the cunt I swive.

The Imperfect Enjoyment

Naked she lay, clasped in my longing arms,
I filled with love, and she all over charms,
Both equally inspired with eager fire,
Melting through kindness, flaming in desire:
With arms, legs, lips, close clinging to embrace,   5
She clips me to her breast, and sucks me to her face.
The nimble tongue (love's lesser lightning) played
Within my mouth, and to my thoughts conveyed
Swift orders, that I should prepare to throw
The all-dissolving thunderbolt below.   10
My fluttering soul, sprung with the pointed kiss,
Hangs hovering o'er her balmy brinks of bliss.
But whilst her busy hand would guide that part,
Which should convey my soul up to her heart,
In liquid raptures I dissolve all o'er,   15
Melt into sperm, and spend at every pore:
A touch from any part of her had done't,
Her hand, her foot, her very look's a cunt.
Smiling, she chides in a kind murmuring noise,
And from her body wipes the clammy joys;   20
When with a thousand kisses, wand'ring o'er
My panting bosom, and 'Is there then no more?'
She cries. 'All this to love and rapture's due;
Must we not pay a debt to pleasure too?'
But I, the most forlorn, lost man alive,   25
To show my wished obedience vainly strive.

I sigh, alas! and kiss, but cannot swive.
Eager desires confound my first intent,
Succeeding shame does more success prevent,
And rage, at last, confirms me impotent.   30
Even her fair hand, which might bid heat return
To frozen age, and make cold hermits burn,
Applied to my dead cinder, warms no more,
Than fire to ashes could past flames restore,
Trembling, confused, limber, dry,   35
A wishing, weak, unmoving lump I lie.
This dart of love, whose piercing point oft tried
With virgin blood, ten thousand maids has dyed;
Which Nature still directed with such art,
That it through every cunt reached every heart.   40
Stiffly resolved, 'twould carelessly invade
Woman or man, nor aught its fury stayed,
Where'er it pierced, a cunt it found, or made.
Now languid lies, in this unhappy hour,
Shrunk up, and sapless, like a withered flower.   45
Thou treacherous, base deserter of my flame,
False to my passion, fatal to my fame;
Through what mistaken magic does thou prove
So true to lewdness, so untrue to love?
What oyster, cinder, beggar, common whore,   50
Didst thou ere fail in all thy life before?
When vice, disease and scandal lead the way,
With what officious haste dost thou obey?
Like a rude roaring hector, in the streets,
That scuffles, cuffs, and ruffles all he meets;   55
But if his king and country claim his aid,
The rakehell villain shrinks, and hides his head:
Even so thy brutal valour is displayed:
Breaks every stew, does each small whore invade,
But when great Love the onset does command,   60
Base recreant to thy prince, thou darest not stand.
Worst part of me, and henceforth hated most
Through all the town: a common fucking-post,
On whom each whore relieves her tingling cunt,
As hogs on goats do rub themselves and grunt   65

May'st thou to ravenous cankers be a prey,
Or in consuming weepings waste away.
May strangury and stone thy days attend,
May'st thou ne'er piss, who did refuse to spend,
When all my joys did on false thee depend.   70
And may ten thousand abler pricks agree
To do the wronged Corinna right for thee.

Translation: from Ovid's *Amores*

O Love! How cold and slow to take my part,
Thou idle wanderer about my heart.
Why thy old faithful, soldier wilt thou see
Oppressed in thy own tents? They murder me.
Thy flames consume, thy arrows pierce thy friends;   5
Rather, on foes pursue more noble ends.
Achilles' sword would generously bestow
A cure as certain as it gave the blow.
Hunters who follow flying game give o'er
When the prey's caught; hope still leads on before.   10
We thine own slaves feel thy tyrannic blows,
Whilst thy tame hand's unmoved against thy foes.
On men disarmed how can you gallant prove?
And I was long ago disarmed by love.
Millions of dull men live, and scornful maids: 15
We'll own Love valiant when he these invades.
Rome from each corner of the wide world snatched
A laurel; or 't had been to this day thatched.
But the old soldier has his resting place,
And the good battered horse is turned to grass.   20
The harassed whore, who lived a wretch to please,
Has leave to be a bawd and take her ease.
For me, then, who have freely spent my blood,
Love, in thy service, and so boldly stood
In Celia's trenches, were 't not wisely done   25
E'en to retire, and live at peace at home?
No! Might I gain a godhead to disclaim

My glorious title to my endless flame,
Divinity with scorn I would forswear,
Such sweet, dear, tempting devils women are.   30
Whene'er these flames grow faint, I quickly find
A fierce black storm pours down upon my mind.
Headlong I'm hurled, like horsemen who in vain
Their fury-foaming coursers would restrain.
As ships, just when the harbour they attain,   35
Are snatched by sudden blasts to sea again,
So Love's fantastic storms reduce my heart
Half-rescued, and the god resumes his dart.
Strike here, this undefended bosom wound,
And for so brave a conquest be renowned.   40
Shafts fly so fast to me from every part,
You'll scarce discern your quiver from my heart.
What wretch can bear a livelong night's dull rest,
Or think himself in lazy slumbers blessed?
Fool! Is not sleep the image of pale death?   45
There's time for rest when Fate has stopped your breath.
Me may my soft deluding dear deceive:
I'm happy in my hopes whilst I believe.
Now let her flatter, then as fondly chide:
Often may I enjoy, oft be denied.   50
With doubtful steps the God of War does move
By thy example led, ambiguous Love.
Blown to and fro like down from thine own wing,
Who knows when joy or anguish thou wilt bring?
Yet at thy mother's and thy slaves' request,   55
Fix an eternal empire in my breast;
And let th' inconstant charming sex,
Whose wilful scorn does lovers vex,
Submit their hearts before thy throne:
The vassal world is then thy own.   60

Phyllis be gentler, I advise

Phyllis be gentler, I advise,
    Make up for time misspent,
When beauty on its death-bed lies,
    'Tis high time to repent.

Such is the malice of your fate, 5
    That makes you old so soon,
Your pleasure ever comes too late,
    How early e'er begun.

Think what wretched thing is she
    Whose stars contrive in spite 10
The morning of her love should be
    Her fading beauty's night.

Then if to make your ruin more
    You'll peevishly be coy,
Die with the scandal of a whore, 15
    And never know the joy.

Mistress Knight's Advice
to the Duchess of Cleveland –
in distress for a prick

Quoth the Duchess of Cleveland to Mistress Knight,
I'd fain have a prick, but how to come by 't?
I desire you'll be secret, and give your advice,
Though cunt be not coy, reputation is nice.

To some cellar in Sodom your Grace must retire, 5
There porters with black pots sit round a coal fire.
There open your case, and your Grace cannot fail
Of a dozen of pricks, for a dozen of ale.

Is't so? quoth the Duchess.

                              Aye by God, quoth the whore.
Then give me the key that unlocks the back door –   10
For I had rather be fucked with porters and car-men,
Than thus be abused by Churchill and Jermyn.

A Session of the Poets

Since the sons of the Muses grew numerous and loud
For the appeasing so factious and clamorous a crowd,
Apollo thought fit, in so weighty a cause,
To establish a government, leader, and laws:
The hopes of the bays, at this summoning call,   5
Had drawn 'em together, the devil and all;
All thronging and listening, they gaped for the blessing,
No presbyter sermon had more crowding and pressing.
In the head of the gang John Dryden appeared,
That ancient grave wit so long loved and feared;   10
But Apollo had heard a story i'th' town
Of his quitting the Muses to wear a black gown;
And so gave him leave, now his poetry's done,
To let him turn priest, now Reeves is turned nun.
This reverend author was no sooner set by   15
But Apollo had got gentle George in his eye;
And frankly confessed, of all men that writ
There's none had more fancy, sense, judgment and wit:
But i'th' crying sin idleness he was so hardened
That his long seven years silence was not to be pardoned.   20
Brawny Wycherley was the next man showed his face,
But Apollo e'en thought him too good for the place;
No gentleman-writer that office should bear,
'Twas a trader in wit the laurel should wear,
As none but a Cit e'er makes a Lord Mayor.   25
Next into the crowd Tom Shadwell does wallow,
And swears by his guts, his paunch, and his tallow,
'Tis he that alone best pleases the age,
Himself and his wife have supported the stage.

Apollo well-pleased with so bonny a lad   30
T'oblige him he told him should be huge glad,
Had he half so much wit as he fancied he had.
However to please so jovial a wit,
And to keep him in humour, Apollo thought fit
To bid him drink on, and keep his old trick   35
Of railing at poets, and showing his prick.
Nat Lee stepped in next, in hopes of a prize,
Apollo remembered he had hit once in thrice;
By the rubies in 's face he could not deny
He had as much wit as wine could supply;   40
Confessed that indeed, he had a musical note,
But sometimes strained so hard that he rattled i'th' throat.
Yet owning he had sense, t'encourage him for't,
He made him his Ovid, in Augustus's court.
Poet Settle, his trial, was the next came about,   45
He brought him an *Ibrahim*, with the preface torn out;
And humbly desired he might give no offence.
'God damn me,' cries Shadwell, 'he cannot write sense.'
'And bollocks,' cried Newport, 'I hate that dull rogue.'
Apollo considering he was not in vogue   50
Would not trust his dear bays with so modest a fool,
And bid the great boy should be sent back to school.
Tom Otway came next, Tom Shadwell's dear zany,
And swears for heroics he writes best of any:
Don Carlos his pockets so amply had filled,   55
That his mange was quite cured, and his lice were all killed.
But Apollo had seen his face on the stage,
And prudently did not think fit to engage
The scum of a play-house for the prop of an age.
In the numerous herd that encompassed him round   60
Little starched Johnny Crowne at his elbow he found;
His cravat-string new-ironed, he gently did stretch
His lily-white hand out the laurel to reach;
Alleging that he had most right to the bays
For writing romances and shiting of plays.   65
Apollo rose up and gravely confessed

Of all men that writ, his talent was best;
For since pain and dishonour man's life only damn
The greatest felicity mankind can claim
Is to want sense of smart, and be past sense of shame: 70
And to perfect his bliss, in poetical rapture,
He bid him be dull, to the end of the chapter.
The poetess Aphra next showed her sweet face,
And swore by her poetry and her black ace
The laurel by a double right was her own,   75
For the plays she had writ and the conquest she had won.
Apollo acknowledged 'twas hard to deny her,
But to deal frankly and ingeniously by her,
He told her, were conquests and charms her pretence,
She ought to have pleaded a dozen years since.   80
At last *Mamamouchi* came in for a share,
And little Tom Essence, author, was there.
Nor could Durfey forbear for the laurel to stickle,
Protesting he had had the honour to tickle
The ears of the town with his dear *Madam Fickle.*   85
With other pretenders whose names I'd rehearse,
But that they're too long to stand in my verse,
Apollo quite tired with their tedious harangue,
Finds at last Tom Betterton, face in the gang,
And since poets without the kind players may hang   90
By his own sacred light he solemnly swore
That in search of a laureate he'd look out no more.
A general murmur ran quite through the hall,
To think that the bays to an actor should fall:
But Apollo to quiet and pacify all   95
E'en told 'em, to put his desert to the test,
That he had made plays as well as the best;
And was the greatest wonder the age ever bore,
For of all the play-scribblers that e'er writ before,
His wit had most worth, and most modesty in't,   100
For he had writ plays yet ne'er came in print.

Upon his leaving his mistress

'Tis not that I am weary grown
Of being yours, and yours alone;
But with what face can I incline
To damn you to be only mine?
You whom some kinder power did fashion,   5
By merit and by inclination,
The joy at least of one whole nation.

Let meaner spirits of your sex,
With humbler aims their thoughts perplex,
And boast, if by their arts they can   10
Contrive to make one happy man;
Whilst moved by an impartial sense,
Favours, like nature, you dispense,
With universal influence.

See the kind seed-receiving earth,   15
To ev'ry grain affords a birth;
On her no showers unwelcome fall,
Her willing womb retains 'em all.
And shall my Celia be confined?
No! Live up to thy mighty mind,   20
And be the mistress of mankind.

On the supposed author
of a late Poem 'In Defence of Satire'

To rack and torture thy unmeaning brain
In satire's praise, to a low, untuned strain,
In thee was most impertinent and vain:
When in thy person we more clearly see
That satire's of divine authority,   5
For God made one on man when he made thee.
To show there are some men, as there are apes,
Framed for mere sport, who differ but in shapes:
In thee are all those contradictions joined
That make an ass, prodigious and refined.   10
A lump deformed and shapeless wert thou born,
Begot in Love's despite, and Nature's scorn;
And art grown up the most ungraceful wight,
Harsh to the ear, and hideous to the sight,
Yet Love's thy business, Beauty thy delight.   15
Curse on that silly hour that first inspired
Thy madness, to pretend to be admired;
To paint thy grizzly face, to dance, to dress,
And all those awkward follies that express
Thy loathsome love, and filthy daintiness.   20
Who needs will be an ugly *beau-garçon*,
Spit at and shunned by every girl in town;
Where dreadfully love's scarecrow thou art placed
To fright the tender flock that long to taste;
While every coming maid, when you appear,   25
Starts back for shame, and straight turns chaste for fear.
For none so poor or prostitute have proved,
Where you made love, t'endure to be beloved.
'Twere labour lost, or else I would advise.
But thy half-wit will ne'er let thee be wise.   30
Half-witty and half-mad, and scarce half-brave,
Half-honest (which is very much a knave).
Made up of all these halves, thou canst not pass
For anything entirely, but an ass.

The Submission

To this moment a rebel I throw down my arms,
Great Love, at first sight of Olinda's fair charms;
Made proud and secure by such forces as these
You may now be a tyrant as soon as you please.

When innocence, beauty, and wit do conspire   5
To betray, and engage, and inflame my desire,
Why should I decline what I cannot avoid,
And let pleasing hope by base fear be destroyed?

Her innocence cannot contrive to undo me,
Her beauty's inclined, or why should it pursue me,   10
And wit has to pleasure been ever a friend,
Then what room for despair, since delight is Love's end?

There can be no danger in sweetness and youth,
Where Love is secured by good-nature and truth;
On her beauty I'll gaze, and of pleasure complain,   15
While every kind look adds a link to my chain.

'Tis more to maintain than it was to surprise,
But her wit leads in triumph the slave of her eyes –
I beheld with the loss of my freedom before,
But hearing, forever must serve and adore.   20

Too bright is my goddess, her temple too weak.
Retire divine image, I feel my heart break.
Help, Love! I dissolve in a rapture of charms
At the thought of those joys I should meet in her arms.

Anacreontic, following Ronsard:
Upon his Drinking a Bowl

Vulcan, contrive me such a cup
   As Nestor used of old;
Show all thy skill to trim it up,
   Damask it round with gold.

Make it so large, that filled with sack,   5
   Up to the swelling brim,
Vast toasts, on the delicious lake,
   Like ships at sea may swim.

Engrave no battle on his cheek
   With war I've nought to do;   10
I'm none of those that took Maastricht,
   Nor Yarmouth Leaguer knew.

Let it no name of planets tell,
   Fixed stars or constellations,
For I am no Sir Sydrophel,   15
   Nor none of his relations.

But carve thereon a spreading vine,
   Then add two lovely boys;
Their limbs in amorous fold entwine,
   The type of future joys.   20

Cupid and Bacchus my saints are,
   May drink and love still reign;
With wine I wash away my cares,
   And then to cunt again.

An Allusion to Horace:
The Tenth Satire of the First Book

Well sir, 'tis granted I said Dryden's rhymes
Were stolen, unequal, nay dull many times:
What foolish patron is there found of his
So blindly partial to deny me this?
But that his plays, embroidered up and down   5
With wit and learning justly pleased the Town
In the same paper I as freely own:
Yet having this allowed, the heavy mass
That stuffs up his loose volumes must not pass:
For by that rule I might as well admit   10
Crowne's tedious scenes for poetry and wit.
'Tis therefore not enough, when your false sense
Hits the false judgment of an audience
Of clapping fools, assembling a vast crowd
Till the thronged play-houses crack with the dull load;   15
Though even that talent merits in some sort
That can divert the rabble and the Court.
Which blundering Settle never could attain,
And puzzling Otway labours at in vain.
But within due proportions, circumscribe   20
Whate'er you write; that with a flowing tide
The style may rise, yet in its rise forbear
With useless words t'oppress the wearied ear.
Here be your language lofty, there more light,
Your rhetoric with your poetry unite: 25
For elegance sake, sometimes allay the force
Of epithets; 'twill soften the discourse;
A jest in scorn points out and hits the thing,
More home than the morosest satire's sting.
Shakespeare and Jonson herein did excel,   30
And might in this be imitated well;
Whom refined Etherege copied not at all,
But is himself a sheer original:
Nor that slow drudge, in swift Pindaric strains,
Flatman, who Cowley imitates with pains,   35
And rides a jaded Muse, whipped with loose reins.

When Lee makes temperate Scipio fret and rave
And Hannibal a whining amorous slave
I laugh, and wish the hot-brained fustian fool
In Busby's hands, to be well-lashed at school.   40
Of all our modern wits, none seems to me
Once to have touched upon true comedy,
But hasty Shadwell, and slow Wycherley.
Shadwell's unfinished works do yet impart
Great proofs of force of nature, none of art.   45
With just bold strokes he dashes here and there,
Showing great mastery with little care;
And scorns to varnish his good touches o'er,
To make the fools and women praise 'em more.
But Wycherley earns hard what he gains,   50
He wants not judgment, nor he spare no pains;
He frequently excels, and at the least,
Makes fewer faults than any of the best.
   Waller, by nature for the bays designed,
With force with fire, and fancy unconfined,   55
In panegyrics does excel mankind;
He best can turn, enforce, and soften things,
To praise great conquerors, or to flatter kings.
   For pointed satires I would Buckhurst choose,
The best good man, with the worst-natured Muse.   60
   For songs and verses, mannerly obscene
That can stir Nature up, by springs unseen,
And without forcing blushes warm the Queen:
Sedley has that prevailing gentle art,
That can with a resistless charm impart   65
The loosest wishes to the chastest heart,
Raise such a conflict, kindle such a fire
Betwixt declining virtue and desire
Till the poor vanquished maid dissolves away
In dreams all night, in sighs and tears all day.   70
   Dryden in vain tried this nice style of wit,
For he, to be a tearing blade thought fit;
But when he would be sharp, he still was blunt,
To frisk his frolic fancy, he'd cry 'cunt';
Would give the ladies a dry bawdy bob,   75
And thus he got the name of Poet Squab:

But to be just, 'twill to his praise be found
His excellencies more than his faults abound.
Nor dare I from his sacred temples tear
That laurel, which he best deserves to wear.   80
But does not Dryden find ev'n Jonson dull?
Fletcher and Beaumont uncorrect and full
Of lewd lines, as he calls 'em? Shakespeare's style
Stiff and affected? To his own the while
Allowing all the justness that his pride   85
So arrogantly had to these denied?
And may not I have leave, impartially
To search, and censure Dryden's works, and try
If those gross faults his choice pen does commit
Proceed from want of judgment, or of wit?   90
Or if his lumpish fancy does refuse
Spirit and grace to his loose slattern Muse?
Five hundred verses every morning writ,
Proves you no more a poet than a wit.
Such scribbling authors have been seen before,   95
Mustapha, *The English Princess*, forty more,
Were things perhaps composed in half an hour.
To write what may securely stand the test
Of being well read over thrice at least,
Compare each phrase, examine every line,   100
Weight every word, and every thought refine;
Scorn all applause the vile rout can bestow
And be content to please those few who know.
Canst thou be such a vain mistaken thing
To wish thy works might make a play-house ring   105
With the unthinking laughter, and poor praise
Of fops and ladies, facetious for thy plays?
Then send a cunning friend to learn thy doom
From the shrewd judges in the drawing-room.
I've no ambition on that idle score,   110
But say with Betty Morris, heretofore,
When a Court Lady called her 'Bulkeley's whore':
'I please one man of wit, am proud on't too,
Let all the coxcombs dance to bed to you.'
Should I be troubled when the purblind knight,   115
Who squints more in his judgment than his sight,

Picks silly faults, and censures what I write?
Or when the poor-fed poets of the Town
For scraps and coach-room cry my verses down?
I loath the rabble – 'tis enough for me   120
If Sedley, Shadwell, Shepherd, Wycherley,
Godolphin, Butler, Buckhurst, Buckingham,
And some few more, whom I omit to name
Approve my sense – I count their censure fame.

To Corinna

What cruel pains Corinna takes
   To force that harmless frown;
When not one charm her face forsakes,
   Love cannot lose his own.

So sweet a face, so soft a heart,   5
   Such eyes so very kind,
Betray, alas, the silly art
   Virtue had ill-designed.

Poor feeble tyrant, who in vain
   Would proudly take upon her,   10
Against kind nature to maintain
   Affected rules of honour.

The scorn she bears so helpless proves,
   When I plead passion to her,
That much she fears (but more she loves)   15
   Her vassal should undo her.

After Boileau

AUDITOR: What Timon, does old age begin t'approach
That thus thou droop'st under a night's debauch?
Hast thou lost deep to needy rogues on tick?
Who ne'er could pay, and must be paid next week?
TIMON: Neither, alas, but a dull, dining sot   5
Seized me i'the Mall, who just my name had got;
He runs upon me, cries, 'Dear rogue, I'm thine,
With me some wits of thy acquaintance dine.'
I tell him I'm engaged, but as a whore
Whose modesty enslaves her spark, the more,   10
The longer I denied, the more he pressed;
At last I e'en consent to be his guest.
He takes me in his coach, and as we go
Pulls out a libel, of a sheet or two –
Insipid as *The Praise of Pious Queens*,   15
Or Shadwell's former unassisted scenes –
Which he admired, and praised at every line;
At last, it was so sharp, it must be mine.
I vowed I was no more a wit than he,
Unpractised, and unblessed in poetry;   20
A song 'To Phyllis' I perhaps might make,
But never rhymed, but for my pintle's sake;
I envied no man's fortune, nor his fame,
Nor ever thought of a revenge so tame.
He knew my style, he swore, and 'twas in vain   25
Thus to deny the issue of my brain.
Choked with his flattery I no answer make,
But silent leave him to his dear mistake,
Which he by this has spread o'er the whole town,
And me with an officious lie undone.   30
Of a well-meaning fool I'm most afraid,
Who sillily reports what was well-said.
But this was not the worst. When he came home
He asked, 'Are Sedley, Buckhurst, Savile, come?'
No, but there were above Halfwit and Huff,   35
Kickum and Dingboy. 'Oh, 'tis well enough.
They're all brave fellows,' cries mine host, 'let's dine,
I long to have my belly full of wine;

They'll write, and fight, I dare assure you,
They're men *tam Marte quam Mercurio*.'   40
I saw my error, but 'twas now too late:
No means, nor hopes appear of a retreat.
Well, we salute, and each man takes his seat.
'Boy,' says my sot, 'is my wife ready yet?'
A wife, good gods! A fop and bullies too!   45
For one poor meal, what must I undergo?
In comes milady, straight; she had been fair,
Fit to give love, and prevent despair.
But age, beauty's incurable disease,
Had left her more desire than power to please.   50
As cocks will strike although their spurs be gone,
She with her old blear eyes to smite began;
Though nothing else, she (in despite of time)
Preserved the affectation of her prime:
However you began, she brought in love,   55
And hardly from that subject would remove.
We chanced to speak of the French King's success;
My lady wondered much how heaven could bless
A man that loved two women at one time;
But more, how he to them excused his crime.   60
She asked Huff if love's flame he never felt?
He answered bluntly – 'Do you think I'm gelt?'
She at his plainness smiled, then turned to me:
'Love, in young minds, precedes even poetry;
You to that passion can no stranger be,   65
But wits are given to inconstancy . . .'
She had run on, I think till now, but meat
Came up, and suddenly she took her seat.
I thought the dinner would make some amends,
When my good host cries out – 'Y'are all my friends.   70
Our own plain fare, and the best tierce The Bull
Affords, I'll give you, and your bellies full;
As for French kickshaws, Sillery and Champoon,
Ragouts and fricassées, in troth we 'ave none.'
Here's a good dinner towards, thought I, when straight 75
Up comes a piece of beef, full horseman's weight,
Hard as the arse of Mosely, under which
The coachman sweats, as ridden by a witch.

A dish of carrots, each of 'em as long
As tool that to fair countess did belong;   80
Which her small pillow could not so well hide
But visitors his flaming head espied.
Pig, goose, and capon followed in the rear,
With all that country bumpkins call 'good cheer':
Served up with sauces, all of Eighty-Eight,   85
When our tough youth wrestled and threw the weight.
And now the bottle briskly flies about,
Instead of ice, wrapped in a wet clout.
A brimmer follows the third bit we eat,
Small beer becomes our drink, and wine our meat.
The table was so large that in less space
A Man might safe six old Italians place;
Each man had as much room as Porter, Blount,
Or Harris had, in Cullen's bushel cunt.
And now the wine began to work: mine host   95
Had been a colonel; we must hear him boast,
Not of towns won, but an estate lost
For the King's service, which indeed he spent
Whoring and drinking, but with good intent.
He talked much of a plot, and money lent   100
In Cromwell's time. My lady she
Complained our love was coarse, our poetry
Unfit for modest ears: small whores and players
Were of our hair-brained youth the only cares;
Who were too wild for any virtuous league,   105
Too rotten to consummate the intrigue.
Falkland she praised, and Suckling's easy pen,
And seemed to taste their former parts again.
Mine host drinks to 'The best in Christendom',
And decently my lady quits the room.   110
Left to ourselves, of several things we prate,
Some regulate the stage, and some the State.
Halfwit cries up my Lord of Orrery,
'Ah how well Mustapha and Zanger die!
His sense so little forced, that by one line   115
You may the other easily divine:
    And which is worse, if any worse can be,
    He never said one word of it to me.

There's fine poetry! You'd swear 'twere prose,
So little on the sense the rhymes impose.'   120
'Damn me,' says Dingboy, 'in my mind, god's-wounds,
Etherege writes airy songs and soft lampoons
The best of any man; as for your nouns,
Grammar, and rules of art, he knows 'em not,
Yet writ two talking plays, without one plot.'   125
Huff was for Settle, and *Morocco* praised,
Said rumbling words, like drums, his courage raised.
 'Whose broad built bulks the boist'rous billows bear,
 Saphee and Salli, Mugadore, Oran,
 The famed Arzille, Alcazar, Tituan . . .   130
Was ever braver language writ by man?'
Kickum for Crowne declared, said, in romance
He had outdone the very wits of France.
'Witness *Pandion*, and his *Charles the Eight*,
Where a young monarch, careless of his fate,   135
Though foreign troops and rebels shook his State,
Complains another sight afflicts him more:
 The Queen's galleys rowing from the shore,
 Fitting their oars and tackling to be gone,
 Whilst sporting waves smiled on the rising sun.   140
Waves smiling on the sun! I'm sure that's new,
And 'twas well thought on, give the devil his due.'
Mine host, who had said nothing in an hour,
Rose up, and praised *The Indian Emperor*:
 As if our old world modestly withdrew,   145
 And here in private had brought forth a new.
'There are two lines! Who but he durst presume
To make the old world a new withdrawing room,
Whereof another world she's brought to bed!
What a brave midwife is a Laureate's head!   150
But pox of all these scribblers, what do'e think,
Will Souches this year any champoon drink?
Will Turenne fight him?' 'Without doubt,' says Huff,
'If they two meet, their meeting will be rough.'
'Damn me,' says Dingboy, 'the French cowards are,   155
They pay, but the English, Scots, and Swiss make war.
In gaudy troops, at a review they shine,
But dare not with the Germans battle join;

What now appears like courage is not so,
'Tis a short pride, which from success does grow;   160
On their first blow, they'll shrink into those fears
They sowed at Crecy, Agincourt, Poitiers;
Their loss was infamous. Honour so stained
Is by a nation not to be regained.'
'What they were then, I know not, now they're brave,   165
He that denies it – lies and is a slave,'
Says Huff, and frowned. Says Dingboy, 'That do I.'
And at that word, at t'other's head let fly
A greasy plate, when suddenly, they all
Together by the ears in parties fall.   170
Halfwit with Dingboy joins, Kickum with Huff;
Their swords were safe, and so we let 'em cuff
Till they, mine host, and I had all enough.
Their rage once over, they begin to treat,
And six fresh bottles must the peace complete.   175
I ran downstairs, with a vow nevermore
To drink beer-glass, and hear the hectors roar.

A Pastoral Dialogue between
Alexis and Strephon

ALEXIS: There sighs not on the plain
                    So lost a swain as I;
                Scorched up with love, frozen with disdain.
                Of killing sweetness I complain.
STREPHON: If 'tis Corinna, die.   5

                Since first my dazzled eyes were thrown
                    On that bewitching face,
                Like ruined birds robbed of their young,
                Lamenting, frighted, and alone,
                    I fly from place to place.   10

Framed by some cruel powers above
    So nice is she, and fair;
None from undoing can remove,
Since all, who are not blind, must love;
    Who are not vain, despair.   15

ALEXIS: The gods no sooner give a grace,
    But fond of their own art
Severely jealous, ever place,
To guard the glories of a face,
    A dragon in the heart.   20

Proud and ill-natured powers they are,
    Who, peevish to mankind,
For their own honour's sake, with care
Make a sweet form divinely fair,
    And add a cruel mind.   25

STREPHON: Since she's insensible of love,
    By honour taught to hate,
If we, forced by decrees above,
Must sensible to beauty prove,
    How tyrannous is fate!   30

ALEXIS: I to the nymph have never named
    The cause of all my pain.
STREPHON: Such bashfulness may well be blamed;
For since to serve we're not ashamed,
    Why should she blush to reign?   35

ALEXIS: But if her haughty heart despise
    My humble proffered one,
The just compassion she denies,
I may obtain from other's eyes;
    Hers are not fair alone.   40

Devouring flames require new food;
    My heart's consumed almost;
New fires must kindle in her blood,
Or mine go out, and that's as good.

STREPHON: Wouldst live, when love is lost!   45
                Be dead before thy passion dies;
                  For if thou shouldst survive,
                What anguish would the heart surprise,
                To see her flames begin to rise,
                  And thine no more alive.   50

ALEXIS: Rather, what pleasure should I meet
                  In my triumphant scorn,
                To see my tyrant at my feet,
                Whilst taught by her, unmoved I sit,
                  A tyrant in my turn.   55

STREPHON: Ungentle shepherd, cease for shame;
                  Which way can you pretend
                To merit so divine a flame,
                Who to dull life make a mean claim,
                  When love is at an end?   60

                As trees are by their bark embraced,
                  Love to the soul doth cling;
                When torn by th' herd's greedy taste,
                Th' injured plants feel they're defaced,
                  That wither in the spring.   65

                My rifled love would soon retire,
                  Dissolving into air,
                Should I that nymph cease to admire,
                Blessed in whose arms I will expire,
                  Or at her feet despair.   70

Injurious charmer of my vanquished heart

NYMPH: Injurious charmer of my vanquished heart,
                Canst thou feel love, and yet no pity know?
                Since of myself from thee I cannot part,
                Invent some gentle way to let me go.

For what with joy thou didst obtain,   5
  And I with more did give,
In time will make thee false and vain,
  And me unfit to live.

SHEPHERD: Frail angel, that would leave a heart forlorn,
             With vain pretence falsehood might therein lie; 10
             Seek not to cast wild shadows o'er your scorn,
             You cannot sooner change than I can die.
                To tedious life I'll never fall,
                Thrown from thy dear loved breast;
                He merits not to live at all   15
                Who cares to live unblessed.

CHORUS: Then let our flaming hearts be joined,
                While in that sacred fire;
                Ere thou prove false, or I unkind,
                Together both expire.   20

My dear mistress has a heart

My dear mistress has a heart,
  Soft as those kind looks she gave me,
When, with love's resistless art
  And her eyes, she did enslave me.
But her constancy's so weak,   5
  She's so wild and apt to wander,
That my jealous heart would break,
  Should we live one day asunder.

Melting joys about her move,
  Killing pleasures, wounding blisses,   10
She can dress her eyes in love,
  And her lips can arm with kisses;
Angels listen when she speaks,
  She's my delight, all mankind's wonder;
But my jealous heart would break,   15
  Should we live one day asunder.

The Dispute

Betwixt Father Patrick and His Highness of late
There happened a strong and a weighty debate,
Religion was the theme – 'tis strange that they two
Should dispute about that which neither of 'em knew!
When I dare boldly say, if the Truth were but known   5
The weakness of Patrick's and the strength of his own,
He'd have called it a madness and much like a curse
To change from a good one to one that is worse.
For if it be true (as some wags make us think)
That a Papist of all his five senses must wink,   10
A man's no more a man when waking than sleeping,
As long as Father Patrick has his senses in keeping.
And sure it's not so, we must all be mistaken
And have lived in a dream and are just now awaken:
For the Father was mighty in word and in reason,   15
He urged not a syllable, but came so in season
That every argument was stronger and stronger,
So the Duke cried at last, 'I can hold out no longer!'
The reasons that moved most his Highness to yield
And so willingly quit to St Patrick the field   20
Were, first, sir, they cheat you and leave you in the lurch
Who tell you there can be any more than one Church;
And next unto that he averred for a certain
No footsteps of ours could be found before Martin.
At which two reasons, so deep and profound   25
The Duke had much ado not to fall in a swound;
But at length he cried out, 'Father Patrick, I find,
By the sudden conversion and change of my mind,
It is not your reason nor wit can afford
Such strength to your cause – 'tis the finger o' th' Lord: 30
For now I remember he somewhere has said
That from babes and from sucklings his truth is conveyed;
And therefore I submit, for my conscience's ease,
To be led by the nose as your Fathership please.'

Thus ends the dispute 'twixt the priest and the knight,   35
In which (to speak truth and to do all sides right)
He managed the cause as he did his sea-fight.

Absent from thee I languish still

Absent from thee I languish still
  Then ask me not when I return?
The straying fool 'twill plainly kill,
  To wish all day, all night to mourn

Dear, from thine arms then let me fly,   5
  That my fantastic mind may prove,
The torments it deserves to try,
  That tears my fixed heart from my love.

When wearied with a world of woe,
  To thy safe bosom I retire,   10
Where love and peace and truth does flow,
  May I contented there expire.

Lest once more wand'ring from that heaven
  I fall on some base heart unblessed;
Faithless to thee, false, unforgiven,   15
  And lose my everlasting rest.

The Mistress

An age in her embraces past,
  Would seem a winter's day;
When life and light, with envious haste,
  Are torn and snatched away.

But, oh how slowly minutes roll,   5
  When absent from her eyes
That feed my love, which is my soul,
  It languishes and dies.

For then no more a soul but shade,
  It mournfully does move;   10

And haunts my breast, by absence made
    The living tomb of love.

You wiser men despise me not;
    Whose love-sick fancy raves,
On shades of souls, and heaven knows what;   15
    Short ages live in graves.

Whene'er those wounding eyes, so full
    Of sweetness, you did see;
Had you not been profoundly dull,
    You had gone mad like me.   20

Nor censure us, you who perceive
    My best-beloved and me,
Sigh and lament, complain and grieve,
    You think we disagree.

Alas! 'Tis sacred jealousy!   25
    Love raised to an extreme;
The only proof 'twixt her and me,
    We love, and do not dream.

Fantastic fancies fondly move,
    And in frail joys believe: 30
Taking false pleasure for true love;
    But pain can ne'er deceive.

Kind jealous doubts, tormenting fears,
    And anxious cares, when past,
Prove our heart's treasure fixed and dear,   35
    And make us blessed at last.

A Song of a Young Lady:
To her Ancient Lover

Ancient Person, for whom I
All the flattering youth defy;
Long be it ere thou grow old,
Aching, shaking, crazy, cold.
But still continue as thou art,   5
   Ancient Person of my heart.

On thy withered lips, and dry,
Which like barren furrows lie;
Brooding kisses I will pour,
Shall thy youthful heat restore.   10
Such kind showers in autumn fall,
And a second spring recall:
Nor from thee will ever part,
   Ancient Person of my heart.

Thy nobler part, which but to name   15
In our sex would be counted shame,
By age's frozen grasp possessed,
From his ice shall be released;
And, soothed by my reviving hand,
In former warmth and vigour stand,   20
All a lover's wish can reach,
For thy joy my love shall teach:
And for thy pleasure shall improve,
All that art can add to love.
Yet still I love thee without art,   25
   Ancient Person of my heart.

A Dialogue between Strephon and Daphne

STREPHON: Prithee now, fond fool, give o'er;
                Since my heart is gone before,
                To what purpose should I stay?
                Love commands another way.

DAPHNE: Perjured swain, I knew the time   5
                When dissembling was your crime.
                In pity now employ that art
                Which first betrayed, to ease my heart.

STREPHON: Women can with pleasure feign:
                Men dissemble still with pain.   10
                What advantage will it prove
                If I lie, who cannot love?

DAPHNE: Tell me then the reason why,
                Love from hearts in love does fly?
                Why the bird will build a nest,   15
                Where he ne'er intends to rest?

STREPHON: Love, like other little boys,
                Cries for hearts, as they for toys:
                Which, when gained, in childish play,
                Wantonly are thrown away.   20

DAPHNE: Still on wing, or on his knees,
                Love does nothing by degrees:
                Basely flying when most prized,
                Meanly fawning when despised.

                Flattering or insulting ever,   25
                Generous and grateful never:
                All his joys are fleeting dreams,
                All his woes severe extremes.

STREPHON: Nymph, unjustly you inveigh;
                Love, like us, must Fate obey.   30

Since 'tis Nature's Law to change,
Constancy alone is strange.

See the heavens in lightnings break,
Next in storms of thunder speak;
Till a kind rain from above   35
Makes a calm – so 'tis in love.

Flames begin our first address,
Like meeting thunder we embrace:
Then you know the showers that fall
Quench the fire, and quiet all.   40

DAPHNE: How should I these showers forget,
'Twas so pleasant to be wet;
They killed love, I knew it well,
I died all the while they fell.

Say at least what nymph it is   45
Robs my breast of so much bliss?
If she's fair I shall be eased,
Through my ruin you'll be pleased.

STREPHON: Daphne never was so fair:
Strephon scarcely so sincere.   50
Gentle, innocent and free,
Ever pleased with only me.

Many charms my heart enthrall,
But there's one above 'em all:
With aversion she does fly   55
Tedious, trading constancy.

DAPHNE: Cruel shepherd! I submit;
Do what love and you think fit:
Change is fate, and not design,
Say you would have still been mine.   60

STREPHON: Nymph, I cannot: 'tis too true,
Change has greater charms than you.

Be, by my example, wise,
Faith to Pleasure sacrifice.

DAPHNE: Silly swain, I'll have to know,   65
'Twas my practice long ago:
Whilst you vainly thought me true,
I was false in scorn of you.

By my tears, my heart's disguise,
I thy love and thee despise.   70
Womankind more joy discovers
Making fools, than keeping lovers.

Translation: from Lucretius

The Gods, by right of Nature, must possess
An everlasting age of perfect peace,
Far off removed from us and our affairs
Neither approached by dangers or by cares,
Rich in themselves, to whom we cannot add,   5
Nor pleased by good deeds, nor provoked by bad.

Grecian Kindness

The utmost grace the Greeks could show
   When to the Trojans they grew kind
Was with their arms to let 'em go,
   And leave their lingering wives behind.
They beat the men and burnt the town,   5
Then all the baggage was their own.

There the kind deity of wine
   Kissed the soft wanton god of love;
This clapped his wings, that pressed his vine,
   And their best powers united move.   10

While each brave Greek embraced his punk,
Lulled her asleep, and then grew drunk.

Insulting Beauty, you misspend

Insulting Beauty, you misspend
   Those frowns upon your slave;
Your scorn against such rebels bend,
Who dare with confidence pretend
That other eyes their hearts defend,   5
   From all the charms you have.

Your conquering eyes so partial are
   Or mankind is so dull,
That while I languish in despair,
Many proud senseless hearts declare   10
They find you not so killing fair,
   To wish you merciful.

They an inglorious freedom boast;
   I triumph in my chain;
Nor am I unrevenged, though lost;   15
Nor you unpunished, though unjust,
When I alone, who love you most,
   Am killed with your disdain.

Rochester's Answer to verses sent him by Lady Betty Felton

What strange surprise to meet such words as these!
Such terms of honour were ne'er chose to please:
To meet, 'midst pleasures of a jovial night
Words that can only give amaze and fright,

No gentle thought that does to love invite.
Were it not better far your arms t'employ   5
Grasping a lover in pursuit of joy,
Than handling sword and pen, weapons unfit:
Your sex gains conquest by their charms and wit.
Of writers slain I could with pleasure hear,   10
Approve of fights, o'erjoyed to cause a tear;
So slain, I mean, that she should soon revive,
Pleased in my arms to find herself alive.

A Familiar Dialogue betwixt Strephon and Sylvia

STREPHON: Sylvia, ne'er despise my love
                   For Colin's mightier dart,
                   My force and vigour you shall prove,
                       Will reach your panting heart.
                   To fools such monsters Nature sends   5
                   For want of brains, a dull amends.

SYLVIA: Content yourself with what you're due.
                   Him you excel in wit, 'tis true,
                   But Colin has his merits too.
                   Wit is but words, and words but wind   10
                   That dallies with a wanton mind.
                   As Zephyr's gentle breezes play,
                   With my extended limbs in May:
                   But you methinks, sweet sir, should know,
                   'Tis substance that prevails below.   15
                   To each then his just dole I'll give,
                   With you I'll talk, with him I'll swive.
                   Your wit shall raise my strong desires,
                   And he shall quench my raging fires.
                   Thus both your merits I'll unite,   20
                   You shall my ear, he please my appetite.

STREPHON: This said, with speed the cursed bitch retired,
    And left me with just indignation fired;
    But taught in women's prostituted schools
    That men of wit but pimp for well-hung fools.   25

After Malherbe:
verses put into a lady's prayer-book

Fling this useless book away,
And presume no more to pray:
Heaven is just, and can bestow
Mercy on none but those that mercy show.
With a proud heart maliciously inclined,   5
Not to increase, but to subdue mankind,
In vain you vex the gods with your petition;
Without repentance and sincere contrition,
You're in a reprobate condition.
Phyllis, to calm the angry powers,   10
And save my soul as well as yours,
Relieve poor mortals from despair,
And justify the gods that made you fair:
And in those bright and charming eyes
   Let pity first appear, then love;   15
   That we by easy steps may rise
Through all the joys on earth to those above.

Verses for which he was Banished

In the Isle of Britain long since famous grown
For breeding the best cunts in all Christendom,
There now does live – ah, let him long survive –
The easiest king and the best bred man alive.
Him no ambition moves to get renown,   10

Like the French fool who wanders up and down
Starving his soldiers, hazarding his crown.
Peace is his aim, his gentleness is such,
And love he loves, for he loves fucking much.
Nor are his high desires above his strength,   10
His sceptre and his prick are of an equal length,
And she that plays with one may play with t'other,
And makes him little wiser than his brother.
The pricks of kings are like buffoons at Court:
We let them rule because they make us sport.   15
He is the sauciest that e'er did swive,
The proudest peremptoriest prick alive.
Whate'er religion or his laws say on't,
He'd break through all to come at any cunt.
Restless he rolls about from whore to whore
A merry monarch, scandalous and poor.
'Oh dearest Carwell, dearest of all dears,
The best relief of my declining years,
Oh how I mourn thy fortune and thy fate,
To love so well and be loved so late!'   25
Yet still his graceless bollocks hung an arse:
Nothing could serve his disobedient tarse.
This to evince were too long to tell ye
The painful chops of his laborious Nelly,
Hands, fingers, arms, mouth, cunt, and thighs,   30
To raise the limb which she each night enjoys.
I hate all monarchs with the thrones they sit on,
From the hector of France to the cully of Britain.

Pindaric

Let ancients boast no more,
Their lewd imperial whore,
Whose everlasting lust
Survived her body's latest thrust;
And when that transitory dust   5

Had no more vigour left in store,
Was still as fresh and active as before.

Her glory must give place,
To one of modern British race;
Whose every daily act exceeds   10
The other's most transcendent deeds:
She has at length made good,
That there is human flesh and blood
Ever able to outdo
All that their loosest wishes prompt 'em to.   15

When she has jaded quite
Her almost boundless appetite,
Cloyed with the choicest banquets of delight,
She'll still drudge on in tasteless vice,
(As if she sinned for exercise)   20
Disabling stoutest stallions every hour,
And when they can perform no more,
She'll rail at 'em, and kick them out of door.

Monmouth and Cavendish droop
As first did Henningham and Scroope;   25
Nay scabby Ned looks thin and pale,
And sturdy Frank himself begins to fail;
But woe betide him if he does,
She'll set her Jockey on his toes
And he shall end the quarrel without blows.   30

Now tell me all ye powers,
Whoe'er could equal this lewd dame of ours?
Laïs herself must yield,
And vanquished Julia quit the field;
Nor can the princess, one day famed   35
As Wonder of the Earth
For Minataur's glorious birth,
With admiration any more be named.
These puny heroines of history
Eclipsed by her shall all forgotten be   40
Whilst her great name confronts Eternity.

Signior Dildo

You ladies all of Merry England
Who have been to kiss the Duchess's hand,
Say did you lately observe in the show
A noble Italian called Signior Dildo?

The Signior was one of her Highness's train   5
And helped to conduct her over the main,
But now she cries out, 'To the Duke I will go,
I have no more need for Signior Dildo.'

At the Sign of the Cross in St James's Street,
When next you go thither to make yourselves sweet,   10
By buying of powder, gloves, essence, or so,
You may chance get a sight of Signior Dildo.

You'll take him at first for no person of note
Because he appears in a plain leather coat:
But when you his virtuous abilities know   15
You'll fall down and worship Signior Dildo.

My Lady Southeske, heaven prosper her for't,
First clothed him in satin, and brought him to Court;
But his head in the circle he scarcely durst show,
So modest a youth was Signior Dildo.   20

The good Lady Suffolk, thinking no harm,
Had got this poor stranger hid under her arm:
Lady Betty by chance came the secret to know,
And from her own mother stole Signior Dildo.

The Countess of Falmouth, of whom people tell   25
Her footmen wear shirts of a guinea an ell,
Might save the expense if she but did know
How lusty a swinger is Signior Dildo.

By the help of this gallant, the Countess of Ralph
Against the fierce Harris preserved herself safe: 30

She stifled him almost beneath her pillow,
So closely she embraced Signior Dildo.

Our dainty fine Duchesses have got a trick
To dote on a fool for the sake of his prick;
The fops were undone did their Graces know   35
The discretion and vigour of Signior Dildo.

That pattern of virtue her Grace of Cleveland
Has swallowed more pricks than the ocean has sand;
But by rubbing and scrubbing so large it does grow,
It is fit for just nothing but Signior Dildo.   40

The Duchess of Modena, though she looks high,
With such a gallant is contented to lie:
And for fear the English her secrets should know,
For a gentleman-usher took Signior Dildo.

The Countess of the Cockpit (who knows not her name?),   45
She's famous in story for a killing dame,
When all her old lovers forsake her, I trow
She'll then be contented with Signior Dildo.

Red Howard, Red Sheldon, and Temple so tall
Complain of his absence so long from Whitehall: 50
Signior Barnard has promised a journey to go,
And bring back his countryman Signior Dildo.

Doll Howard no longer with his Highness must range,
And therefore is proffered this civil exchange:
Her teeth being rotten, she smells best below,   55
And needs must be fitted for Signior Dildo.

St Albans with wrinkles and smiles in his face,
Whose kindness to strangers becomes his high place,
In his coach and six horses is gone to Pergo,
To take the fresh air with Signior Dildo.   60

Were this Signior but known to the citizen fops,
He'd keep their fine wives from the foremen of their shops,

But the rascals deserve their horns should still grow,
For burning the Pope, and his nephew Dildo.

Tom Killigrew's wife, North Holland's fine flower,   65
At the sight of this signior did fart and belch sour;
And her Dutch breeding farther to show,
Says, 'Welcome to England, Myn Heer Van Dildo.'

He civilly came to the Cockpit one night,
And proffered his service to fair Madam Knight,   70
Quoth she, 'I intrigue with Captain Cazzo,
Your nose in mine arse, good Signior Dildo.'

This signior is sound, safe, ready, and dumb,
As ever was candle, carrot, or thumb;
Then away with these nasty devices and show   75
How you rate the just merits of Signior Dildo.

Count Cazzo, who carries his nose very high,
In passion did swear that his rival should die;
Then shut himself up, to let the world know,
Flesh and blood could not bear it from Signior Dildo.   80

A rabble of pricks who were welcome before,
Now finding the porter denied 'em the door,
Maliciously waited his coming below,
And inhumanely fell on Signior Dildo.

Nigh wearied out the poor stranger did fly,   85
And along the Pall Mall, they followed full cry,
The women concerned from every window,
Cried, 'Oh for heaven's sake save Signior Dildo!'

The good Lady Sandys burst into a laughter,
To see how the bollocks came wobbling after,   90
And had not their weight retarded the foe
It had gone hard with Signior Dildo.

Clanbrazil and Fox

Too long the wise Commons have been in debate
About money and conscience (those trifles of State)
Whilst dangerous grievances daily increase,
And the subject can't riot in safety and peace.
Unless (as against Irish cattle before)   5
You now make an act to forbid Irish whore.
The Cootes black and white, Clanbrazil and Fox,
Invade us with impudence, beauty, and pox.
They carry a fate which no man can oppose;
The loss of his heart, and the fall of his nose.   10
Should he dully resist, yet would each take upon her,
To beseech him to do it, and engage him in honour.
Oh ye merciful powers, who of mortals take care,
Make the women more modest, more sound, or less fair.
Is it just, that with Death cruel Love should conspire,   15
And our tarses be burned by our hearts taking fire?
There's an end of communion, if humble believers
Must be damned in the cup, like unworthy receivers.

The Maidenhead

Have you not in a chimney seen
A sullen faggot wet and green,
How coyly it received the heat,
And at both ends does fume and sweat?

So goes it with the harmless maid   5
When first upon her back she's laid;
But the well-experienced dame,
Cracks and rejoices in the flame.

Anacreontic

The heavens carouse each day a cup,
No wonder Atlas holds them up.
The trees suck up the earth and ground,
And in their brown bowls drink around
The sea too, whom the salt makes dry,   5
His greedy thirst to satisfy
Ten thousand rivers drinks, and then
Grows drunk, and spews 'em up again.
The sun (and who so right as he)
Sits up all night to drink the sea.   10
The moon quaffs up the sun her brother,
And wishes she could tope another.
Everything fuddles: then that I,
Is't any reason, should be dry?
Well, I'll be content to thirst,   15
But too much drink shall make me first.

Attempting to kiss the Duchess of Cleveland

*As she was stepping out of her chariot at Whitehall Gate,
she threw Rochester on his back, and before he rose he
spoke the following lines:*

By heavens! 'Twas bravely done
First to attempt the chariot of the sun
And then to fall like Phæton.

On the King

God bless our good and gracious King
    Whose promise none relies on.
Who never said a foolish thing,
    Nor ever did a wise one.

After Quarles
To his Mistress

Why do'st thou shade thy lovely face? Oh why
Does that eclipsing hand of thine deny
The sunshine of the sun's enlivening eye?

Without thy light, what light remains in me?
Thou art my life, my way's my light in thee,   5
I live, I move and by thy beams I see.

Thou art my life, if thou but turn away
My life's a thousand deaths, thou art my way.
Without thee (love) I travel not, but stray.

My light thou art, without thy glorious sight   10
My eyes are darkened with eternal light.
My love thou art my way, my life, my light.

Thou art my way I wander if thou fly
Thou art my light, if hid how blind am I
Thou art my life if thou withdraw I die.   15

My eyes are dark and blind, I cannot see
To whom or whether should my darkness flee
But to that light and who's that light but thee.

If that be all, shine forth and draw thou nigher.

Let me be bold and die for my desire,   20
A Phœnix likes to perish in the fire.

If my puffed light be out, give leave to –
My shameless snuff at the bright lamp of thine
Ah! What's thy light the less for lighting mine.

If I have lost my path, dear lover say.   25
Shall I still wander in a doubtful way?
Love, shall a lamb of Israel's sheepfold stray?

My path is lost, my wandering steps do stray,
I cannot go, nor safely stay.
Whom should I seek but thee – my path, my way.   30

And yet thou turn'st thy face away and fliest me,
And yet I sue for grace, and thou deniest me.
Speak, art thou angry love, or triest me.

Display those heavenly lamps, or tell me why
Thou shadest thy face? Perhaps no eye   35
Can view their flames, and not drop down and die.

Thou art the pilgrim's path and blind-man's eye,
The dead man's life, on thee my hopes rely.
If I but them remove I e'er, I die.

Dissolve thy sunbeams, close thy wings and stay.   40
See, see how I am blind and dead, and stray.
Oh thou that art my life, my light, my way.

Then work my will if passion bid me flee.
My reason shall obey. My wings shall be
Stretched out no further than from me to thee.   45

Extempore to a Country Clerk: after having heard him sing psalms

Sternhold and Hopkins had great qualms
When they translated David's psalms,
   To make the heart full glad:
But it had been poor David's fate
To hear thee sing and them translate   5
   By God 'twould have made him mad.

A Dream

'Twas when the sable mantle of the night
O'erlaid the day, and checked declining light,
'Twas when the raven and the owl begins
To make men's conscience tremble for their sins:
I then methought went armed to my dear,   5
Ready to pay what I had promised her.
I went and found her prostrate in her bed,
Only her smock covering her maidenhead;
I took it up – sweet linen, by your favour –
But oh! How my moist fingers then did savour!   10
I looked, and saw the blind boy's happy cloister,
Arched on both sides, and gaping like an oyster;
I had a tool before me, which I put
Up to the quick, and then the oyster shut.
It shut, and clung so fast at every stroke,   15
As does the loving ivy to the oak;
I thrust it hard, and still was in some hope;
The liquor came, but yet it would not ope;
And then I fainted; but at second bout
It opened, and made way to let me out.   20
It gaped, and would have made a dead man skip
To see it wag and mump its upper lip.
Then fainting lay, and dreamed I was in pain:
I felt my belly wet, and slept again.

Lines written under Nelly's picture

She was so exquisite a whore
That in the belly of her mother
She placed her cunt so right before
Her father fucked them both together.

Rhyme to 'Lisbon'

A health to Kate
Our sovereign's mate
Of the Royal house of Lisbon.
But the devil take Hyde
And the bishop beside,   5
Who made her bone his bone.

On Louis XIV

Lorraine he stole, by fraud he got Burgundy;
Flanders he bought, 'ods you shall pay for it one day.

Here's Monmouth the witty

Here's Monmouth the witty!
And Lauderdale the pretty!
   And Frazier that learned physician!
But above all the rest
Here's the Duke for a jest!   5
   And the King for a grand politician!

To his more than meritorious wife

I am by Fate slave to your will,
And I will be obedient still,
To show my love I will compose ye,
For your fair finger's ring a poesie,
In which shall be expressed my duty,   5
And how I'll be forever true t'ye,
With low-made legs and sugared speeches,
Yielding to your fair bum the breeches,
And show myself in all I can
Your very humble servant,   10

                                        John.

from Mistress Price
to Lord Chesterfield

My lord,
   These are the gloves that I did mention
Last night, and 'twas with the intention
That you should give me thanks and wear them,
For I most willingly can spare them.
When you this packet first do see   5
'Damn me,' cry you, 'she has writ to me
I had better be at Bretby still
Than troubled with love against my will.
Besides this is not all my sorrow
She writ today, she'll come tomorrow.'   10
Then you consider the adventure
And think you never shall content her.
But when you do the inside see
You'll find things are but as they should be,
And that 'tis neither love nor passion   15
But only for your recreation.

The Platonic Lady

I could love thee till I die,
  Wouldst thou love me modestly,
And ne'er press, whilst I live,
  For more than willingly I would give;
    Which should sufficient be to prove   5
    I'd understand the art of love.

I hate the thing is called enjoyment,
  Besides it is a dull employment,
It cuts off all that's life and fire,
  From that which may be termed desire.   10
    Just like the bee whose sting is gone,
    Converts the owner to a drone.

I love a youth will give me leave
  His body in my arms to wreath;
To press him gently and to kiss,   15
  To sigh and look with eyes that wish.
    For what if I could once obtain,
    I would neglect with flat disdain.

I'd give him liberty to toy
  And play with me, and count it joy.   20
Our freedom should be full complete,
  And nothing wanting but the feat:
    Let's practise then, and we shall prove,
    These are the only sweets of love.

Could I but make my wishes insolent

Could I but make my wishes insolent
And force some image of a false content?
But they, like me, bashful and humble grown,
Hover at a distance about Beauty's throne,
Thee worship and admire, and then they die –   5

Daring no more lay hold of her than I.
Reason to worth bears a submissive spirit,
But fools can be familiar with merit.
Who but the blundering blockhead Phæton
Could e'er have thought to drive about the sun.   10
Just such another durst make love to you
Whom not ambition led, but dullness drew.
No amorous thought would his dull heart incline
But he would have a passion, for 'twas fine.
That, a new suit, and what he next must say,   15
Runs in his idle head the live-long day.
Hard-hearted saint, since 'tis your will to be
So unrelenting, pitiless to me,
Regardless of a love so many years
Preserved, 'twixt lingering hopes and awful fears.   20
Such fears in lovers' breasts high value claims,
And such expiring martyrs feel in flames.
My hopes yourself contrived with cruel care,
Through gentle smiles to lead me to despair.
'Tis some relief, in my extreme distress,   25
My rival is below your power to bless.

'Twas a dispute 'twixt Heaven and Earth

'Twas a dispute 'twixt Heaven and Earth
    Which had produced the nobler birth:
For Heaven appeared Cynthia, with all her train,
    Till you came forth,
    More glorious and more worth,   5
Than she with all those trembling imps of light,
    With which this envious Queen of Night
    Had proudly decked her conquered self in vain.

I must have perished in that first surprise,
    Had I beheld your eyes;   10
Love, like Apollo, when he would inspire
    Some holy breast, laid all his glories by.

Else the god clothed in his heavenly fire
Would have possessed too powerfully,
   And making of his priest a sacrifice   15
   Had so returned unhallowed to the skies.

After Jonson

Leave this gaudy gilded stage
From custom more than use frequented
Where fools of either sex and age
Crowd to see themselves presented.
To Love's theatre, the bed,   5
Youth and beauty fly together,
And act so well, it may be said
The laurel there was due to either.
'Twixt strifes of Love and War the difference lies in this:
When neither overcomes, Love's triumph greater is.   10

Sab. Lost

She yields, she yields, pale Envy said 'Amen',
The first of women to the last of men.
Just so those frailer beings angels fell:
There's no midway (it seems) 'twixt heaven and hell.
Was it your end, in making her, to show   5
Things must be raised high to fall so low?
Since her nor angels their own worth secures,
Look to it Gods! The next turn must be yours,
You who in careless scorn laugh at the ways
Of humble love and call 'em rude essays.   10
Could you submit to let this heavy thing
Artless and witless, no way meriting?

Translation: from Lucretius

Great mother of Aeneas and of Love;
Delight of mankind, and the powers above;
Who all beneath those sprinkled drops of light
Which slide upon the face of gloomy night,
Whither vast regions of that liquid world　　　　　5
Where groves of ships on watery hills are hurled,
Or fruitful earth, dost bless, since 'tis by thee
That all things live which the bright sun does see.

– To form a plot

——To form a plot
The blustering bard whose rough unruly rhyme
Gives Plutarch the lie in every line,
Who rapture before nature does prefer,
And now himself turned his own imager,　　　　　5
Defaceth God's in every character.

Fragment of a Satire on Men

What vain unnecessary things are men,
How well we do without 'em, tell me then?
Whence comes that mean submissiveness we find
This ill-bred age has wrought on womankind,
Fallen from the rights their sex and beauties gave　　　　　5
To make men wish and humbly crave?
Now 'twill suffice if they vouchsafe to have
To the Pall Mall, playhouse, and the drawing-room –
Their women-fairs – these women-coursers come,
To chaffer, choose, and ride their bargains home.　　　　　10
At the appearance of an unknown face

Up steps the arrogant pretending ass,
Pulling by the elbow his companion Huff,
Cries, 'Lookee, by God that wench is well enough,
Fair and well-shaped, good lips and teeth – 'twill do: 15
She shall be tawdry for a month or two
At my expense; be rude and take upon her,
Show her contempt of quality and honour,
And with the general fate of errant woman,
Be very proud awhile, then very common.'   20
Ere bear this scorn, I'd be shut up at home,
Content with humouring myself alone,
Force back the humble love of former days
In pensive madrigals and ends of plays,
When if my Lady frowned, th' unhappy knight   25
Was fain to fast and lie alone that night;
But whilst th' insulting wife the breeches wore,
The husband took his clothes to give his whore,
Who now maintains it with a gentler art:
Thus tyrannies to commonwealths convert.   30
Then after all you find, whate'er we say,
Things must go on in their lewd natural way.
Besides the beastly men we daily see
Can please themselves alone as well as we.
Therefore kind Ladies of the Town to you   35
For our stolen ravished men we hereby sue.
By this time you have found out, we suppose,
That they're as arrant tinsel as their clothes.
Poor broken properties that cannot serve
To treat such persons so as they deserve.   40
Mistake us not, we do not here pretend
That like the young sparks, you can condescend
To love a beastly playhouse creature – foh!
We dare not think so meanly of you – no.
'Tis not the player pleases but the part: 45
She make like Rollo who despises Hart.
To theatres as temples you are brought,
Where Love is worshipped, and his precepts taught.
You must go home and practise, for 'tis here,
Just as in other preaching places, where   50
Great eloquence is shown 'gainst sin, and Papists

By men who live idolaters and atheists.
These two were dainty trades, indeed could each
Live up to half the miracles they teach,
Both are a ———   55

Upon Carey Frazier

Her father gave her dildos six;
Her mother made 'em up a score:
But she loves nought but living pricks,
And swears by God she'll frig no more.

And after singing Psalm the Twelfth

And after singing Psalm the Twelfth
He laid his book upon the shelf
And looked much simply like himself;
With eyes turned up as white as ghost
He cried, 'Ah lard, ah lard of hosts!   5
I am a rascal, that thou knowest.'

Against Marriage

Out of mere love and arrant devotion,
Of marriage I'll give you this galloping notion:
It's the bane of all business, the end of all pleasure,
The consumption of youth, wit, courage, and treasure.
It's the rack of our thoughts, and the nightmare of sleep,   5
That sets us to work before the day peep.
It makes us make brick without stubble or straw,

And a cunt has no sense of conscience or law.
If you'd use flesh in the way that is noble,
In a generous wench there is nothing of trouble.   10
You go on, you come off, say, do what you please –
The worst you can fear is but a disease;
And diseases, you know, do admit of a cure,
But the hell-fire of marriage, none can endure.

To the Post-boy

Son of a whore, God damn you, can you tell
A peerless peer the readiest way to Hell?
I've outswilled Bacchus, sworn of my own make
Oaths would fright Furies and make Pluto quake.
I've swived more whores more ways than Sodom's walls 5
E'er knew, or the College of Rome's Cardinals.
Witness heroic scars, look here, ne'er go,
Cerecloths and ulcers from the top to toe.
Frighted at my own mischiefs I have fled
And bravely left my life's defender dead.   10
Broke houses to break chastity, and dyed
That floor with murder which my lust denied.
Pox on it, why do I speak of these poor things?
I have blasphemed my God and libelled Kings;
The readiest way to hell, come quick –   15
BOY: Ne'er stir,
The readiest way, my lord, 's by Rochester.

Dialogue

NELL:	When to the King I bid good-morrow
	With tongue in mouth and hand on tarse,
	Portsmouth may rend her cunt for sorrow,
	And Mazarine may kiss mine arse.

PORTSMOUTH: When England's monarch's on my belly   5
                     With prick in cunt, though double-crammed,
                     Fart of mine arse for small whore Nelly,
                     And great whore Mazarine be damned.

KING: When on Portsmouth's lap I lay my head
            And Knight does sing her bawdy song,   10
            I envy not George Porter's bed
            Nor the delights of Madam Long.

PEOPLE: Now heavens preserve our faith's defender,
             From Paris plots and Roman cunt,
             From Mazarine, that new pretender,   15
             And from that politic Grammont.

On his Prick

Base mettle hanger by thy master's thigh,
Shame and disgrace to all prick heraldry,
Hide thy despised head and do not dare
To peep, no not so much as take the air
But through a buttonhole, but pine and die,   5
Confined within thy codpiece monastery.
The little childish boy that scarcely knows
The channel through which his water flows,
Touched by mistress's most magnetic hand
His little needle presently will stand,   10
And turn to her; but thou, in spite of that,
As oft cocks flopping like an old wife's hat.
Did she not take you in her ivory hand?

Doubtless stroked thee, yet thou would not stand?
Did she not raise thy drooping head on high   15
As it lay nodding on her wanton thigh?
Did she not clasp her legs about thy back,
Her porthole open? Prick, what didst thou lack?
Henceforth stand stiff, regain thy credit lost,
Or I'll ne'er draw thee but against a post.   20

Ad Regem Carolum II

Bellas fugis, Bellas sequeris, Belloque repugnas,
  Et Bellatori sunt tibi Bella Tori.
    Imbelles imbellis amas; audaxque videris
Mars ad opus Veneris, Martis ad arma Venus.

A Curse on his Pintle

Bless me ye stars! For sure some sad portent
Is threatened to me by this sad event
I had a girl, fair well-attired and sweet,
Merry and buxom, for embraces meet.
At my request she laid herself down low,   5
Her legs stretched wide, her cunt to me did show,
In full proportion, pretty mumping thing,
A companion and play-fellow for a king.
Then credit me, for true is my report,
It prettily mouthed and mewed to have me sport.   10
But yet my base, my base unworthy prick
(Base I must term it, for so base a trick)
Lay in despite of me as one stark dead.
I could by no means make him raise his head.
I kissed, I toyed, I clasped her cheeks and tail,   15
And fingered too, yet I could not prevail.

Yea, though she took it in her warm moist hand
And crammed it in, dull dog, it would not stand.

Oh what damned age do we live in

Oh what damned age do we live in
Since there is no Christian soul
But old Father Patrick and Griffin
Dare put their pricks in the right hole.

Oh why do we keep such a bustle   5
'Bout putting a prick in an arse,
Since Harvey's long-cunted muscle
Serves Stuart instead of a tarse.

Since fucking is not as 'twas wont
The ladies have got a new trick: 10
As an arsehole serves for a cunt,
So a clitoris serves for a prick.

Besides, the damned tailors of France
To Great Britain's defamation
Have made better pintles by chance   15
Than the gods of the English nation.

But now there's nothing will do,
Their cunts are grown so wide,
Except with a French leather dildo
They get on each other and ride.   20

A New Ballad to the Tune of Chevy Chase

The parsons all keep whores
In these most blessed times;
The sextons they make bawdy songs,
And set 'em to their chimes.

> *Chorus*
> A pox on formal fops   5
> That former ages praise,
> And always prate of Eighty-Eight,
> And Good Queen Bess's days.

Each prentice now keeps wenches
That ne'er before wore cuffs,   10
And aldermen in Whetstone's Park
Do rumple all their ruffs.
  And a pox on &c

The mayor of London town
Is flogged by his own sheriffs;
The bishops bugger up and down,   15
And all beshit their sleeves.
  And a pox on &c

The City wives have turned Cheapside
Into a damned Pell Mell:
They whore as oft and drink as drunk
As Stuart and Carwell.   20
  And a pox on &c

Our good Lord Chancellor
With his pale meagre face
Does with his bollocks like his purse
And his prick like to his mace.
  And a pox on &c

Even in the House of Peers   25
If he a wench should lack,
He'll take and fuck a judge's arse

Upon his woolly sack.
    And a pox on &c

And God bless Charles the Second
And send him long to reign.   30
For when he's gone 'tis ten to one
We'll ne'er have the like again.
    And a pox on &c

And God bless handsome Kate,
And God bless pious James,
And God bless Gilbert of Canterbury   35
That fucks beyond the Thames.
    And a pox on &c

Heavens bless the clergy too
Their mitres and their copes;
And God bless my good Lord Hawley's bulls,
And the devil confound the Pope's.   40
    And a pox on &c

May members still sell votes
And keep their country poor,
And the taxes raised to kill our friends
Be spent on rogues and whores.
    And a pox on &c

Till Charles do mind his own affairs,   45
And Kate forget to paint,
And Arlington refuse a bribe
And blind Lord Vaughan turn saint.
    And a pox on &c

Notes

p. 3 *Impia blasphemi sileant convitia vulgi* Like the poem which follows, these lines in Latin are attributed to Rochester in a collection of university verses lamenting the death from smallpox of Princess Mary of Orange. **Translation:** Let the graceless gatherings of the scandal-mongering crowd be silent. I acquit the doctors and their ineffective skill. Let medicine treat other diseases with easy drugs. When such sores appear, that art has no strength: a pustule of any kind is a lethal wound to the female face, and kills beauty more surely than a sword. If on the other hand a slighter infection should mark a gentle face, a woman may perhaps escape, but a goddess cannot. In one who is all loveliness, body and soul are equal: how then could she survive?

p. 32 *All this have I with indignation hurled* First published in 1680 as a continuation of 'A Satire against Mankind' but not included in the 1679 broadsheet printing of the 'Satire' which circulated during Rochester's lifetime. While roughly half of the early manuscripts include these lines with the 'Satire' – either as a continuation or under the title 'Addition' – roughly half omit them. Why and when lines to soften the nihilism of the 'Satire' were devised – and whether by Rochester or by some other hand – remains unresolved.

p. 109 *Bella fugis, Bellas sequeris, Belloque repugnas* These four lines of cleverly punning Latin translate literally as follows: *You avoid war* (bella), *you chase fine women* (bellas), *and you flee from confrontation* (bello), *and your preferred battlefields* (bellatori) *are the beds of the fair* (bella tori). *Yourself a pacifist* (imbellis), *you love the unresisting* (imbelles); *and you hold that Mars is brave in the pursuits of Venus, Venus ready for the arms of Mars.*

Index of First Lines